THE Storyteller

MY YEARS WITH

Ernest Thompson Seton

INCLUDING ILLUSTRATIONS AND EXCERPTS FROM HIS STORIES

THE Storyteller

MY YEARS WITH

Ernest Thompson Seton

INCLUDING ILLUSTRATIONS AND EXCERPTS
FROM HIS STORIES

BY **Leila Moss Knox**

WITH **Linda L. Knox**

FOREWORD BY **Pete Seeger**

LANGDON
STREET PRESS

*This book is dedicated to the memory of
my husband David,
with whom I was fortunate to spend more than sixty wonderful years.*

Photo of peacock tile on the wall of Seton Castle

WITH THANKS

To the late folksinger and songwriter Pete Seeger for writing the foreword to this book. Words cannot possibly express my gratitude. Meeting Pete and listening to him speak about his love of Seton's books and the impact Seton's writings had on him will remain a lasting memory.

To my son Jim for his editorial, design, and technical advice.

To my nephew Michael Harrison Tyrrell who accompanied me on several research trips to New Mexico and also created several illustrations for the book.

To Julie Seton, granddaughter of Julia and Ernest Thompson Seton. I am certain they would be pleased that Julie and I have finally met and formed what I hope will be a lasting friendship. My thanks to her and the Seton Family Trust for the use of the Seton Castle drawing.

To art historian, museum curator, and author David L. Witt who so generously gave his time and professional expertise throughout the writing of this book.

To the Academy for the Love of Learning for allowing paintings and drawings from the Seton Gallery and Archives to be used in *The Storyteller.*

To Mai Qaraman, Research Services Librarian at the American Museum of Natural History in New York, for her kindness and helpfulness while Linda and I were reading the Seton journals.

To Robin Taylor of the Seton Memorial Library, Philmont Scout Ranch, for sharing her considerable knowledge of the Seton Collection.

To the countless others who provided assistance during our research and granted us permissions to use text excerpts and photographs.

And finally, to all my children for their love and encouragement in this endeavor. Each of them read and re-read draft after draft of the book, suggested changes, and, as they did to my life, made it better than it otherwise would have been.

CONTENTS

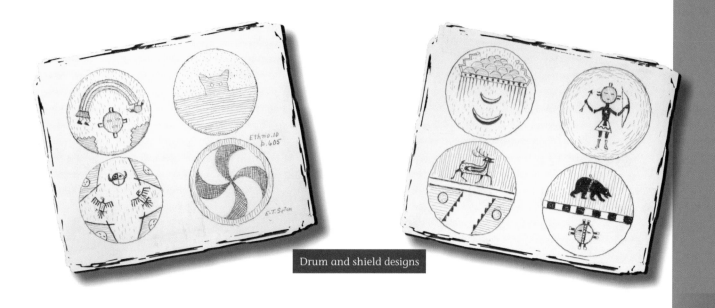

Drum and shield designs

FOREWORD

The influences of Ernest Thompson Seton (1860–1946) on my life can be traced back to my childhood. As a youth, I read every one of his children's books. I remember fondly my favorites: *Rolf in the Woods* and *Two Little Savages.* From his designs, I built a teepee and camped out in the cow pasture. I cooked my meals over a small fire in the teepee as I tried to replicate the life and experiences described in his stories. Seton's love of the outdoors and his respect for the environment inspired me as a youth and have left a lasting impression on me.

Ernest Thompson Seton was co-founder of the Boy Scouts of America and one of our country's original conservationists. Remarkably, he was also an exceptional writer, artist, and storyteller. Since Seton's first book, *Wild Animals I Have Known*, appeared in print in 1898, countless people—young and old—have enjoyed his stories. Many have read his books to their own children, as I did. I am optimistic this book will inspire a continuation of this tradition.

The Storyteller is written by a woman remembering three years of her childhood in the mid-1930s, living in New Mexico with Seton. It provides rare insight into this extraordinary man and his inspirational life.

—*Pete Seeger*

PARTIAL LISTING OF HONORS & AWARDS ACCORDED SETON

1879   Scholarship, Royal Academy of Arts, London, England

1891   Painting "The Sleeping Wolf" featured in the Paris Salon, France

1892   Appointed Provincial Naturalist, Government of Manitoba, Canada
       Served in this capacity until his death in 1946

1893   Painting "Triumph of the Wolves" featured at the Chicago World's Fair

1926   Silver Buffalo Award, Boy Scouts of America
       "This award is Scouting's highest commendation to
       the invaluable contributions that
       outstanding Americans make to youth."

1927   John Burroughs Medal,
       American Museum of Natural History
       "Awarded to the author of a distinguished
       book of natural history" for *Lives of Game
       Animals*

1928   Daniel Giraud Elliot Medal,
       National Institute of Science
       "Awarded for meritorious work in zoology or
       paleontology" for *Lives of Game Animals*

1968   Inducted in the Conservation Hall of Fame,
       National Wildlife Federation

Portrait of Ernest Thompson Seton

PROLOGUE

When I was a little girl, I lived in a castle. The castle belonged to my aunt and uncle, Julia Moss Seton and Ernest Thompson Seton. Although they weren't a king and queen, they were quite famous. Both were well-known writers. My uncle was also a gifted wildlife artist, a renowned naturalist, and an early conservationist. His deep love of nature, his great respect for the traditions of Native American cultures, and his desire to share both with children led him to establish the League of Woodcraft Indians. Some years later, he became a founding member and first Chief Scout of the Boy Scouts of America. More than anything else, however, my uncle was a mesmerizing storyteller.

Seton drawing of the Castle, 1935

Seton Castle stood on a hill majestically overlooking Seton Village, the 2,500 acres of land on the outskirts of Santa Fe, New Mexico that was owned by my aunt and uncle. It was a spacious stone dwelling with thirty-two rooms, a tall tower, and a vast library that held almost 70,000 books and several hundred paintings and drawings. My uncle had designed the castle to reflect the American Southwest, so its exterior in many ways resembled an Indian pueblo.

During the 1930s, I spent three years of my childhood living at Seton Castle with my aunt and uncle. This is the story of my adventures there.

Los Angeles, California

Dear Julie,

I hope you and Seton are well. Pat and I are doing fine, but our little Leila has been very sick. The doctor said we must find a way to send her to a dry climate, away from the city air in Los Angeles. We are so worried about her and have been trying to figure out what we can do.

I was wondering if Leila might stay with you and Seton in New Mexico for a while. The doctor agrees that the air in Santa Fe would be so much healthier for her. We are sure it would help her recover.

Leila is a cheerful little six-year-old. She talks a lot, but she is an enthusiatic student. I don't think she will be any trouble. Would this be possible? If it is, I can drive her to New Mexico whenever you say. Pat and I hope you will be able to help us.

With love,
Your brother,

Lou

Seton Villiage
Santa Fe, New Mexico

Dear Lou,

How good to hear from you. Seton and I have talked it over. We would love to have Leila come and stay with us for as long as it takes her to get better.

No need for you to drive all the way to New Mexico. Just bring Leila as far as Needles on the seventeenth of this month. I'll meet you in front of the post office about 3:00. We can have an early dinner, and then I'll take her back to Santa Fe with me.

I look forward to spending a couple of hours with you.

Much love,
Julie

CHAPTER 1

From Los Angeles to Santa Fe

I was only six the day my father drove us across California to Needles, near the California–Nevada–Arizona border, and delivered me to his sister, my Aunt Julie. My mother had packed peanut butter and jelly sandwiches, apples, and gingersnap cookies for us to eat on our trip. She handed me my lunch bag, and then, hugging me tightly, said her good-byes, explaining again that going to Santa Fe was "doctor's orders"—I needed a drier climate so that my throat and chest could heal properly. Although she had tried not to cry, tears had trickled down her face onto my neck as she held me. My father finally had to pry away her encircling arms so that he and I could start our journey.

I had never been away from home before, and now I was going to live with an aunt and uncle I had never met in a place far from Los Angeles. "Please," I begged my mother, "please don't send me away. I'll be good. I'll try really hard to get well."

"This isn't about being good," she replied. "It's just that the air in New Mexico is healthier. It will help you get better."

I ran to my older sister and grabbed her hand tightly. "Don't let them send me away, Doris. Tell them you'll take care of me. I won't be any trouble!"

Doris knelt down and put her arms around me, rocking me back and forth. Her face was wet with tears. "You have to go, Leila. The doctor says the air in Los Angeles is not good for your throat. It won't be for long, and I promise I'll write to you every day."

"Lou, do you think this is the right thing to try?" My mother was wavering, changing her mind. "She's doing a little better. Can't we just keep her here?" She was going to let me stay.

"Pat, we've been over and over this. This isn't easy for me either. You know she needs to go." My father was starting to sound exasperated. He picked me up and placed me in the passenger seat of the car. Without another sound, he got in on the driver's side and started the engine. I could hear my mother sobbing. I knelt on the seat of the car, waving and throwing kisses to her and my sister and brother. I did not know when, if ever, I would see them again.

When I stopped crying and finally began to pay attention to my surroundings, I realized that the landscape had changed dramatically as my father and I had traveled down the highway—from a busy city to mile after mile of sparsely populated land. The longer we were on the road, the

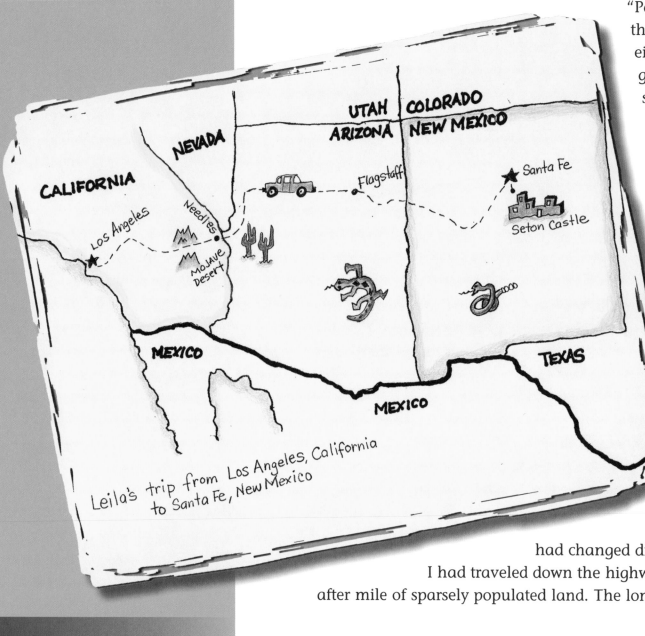

Leila's trip from Los Angeles, California to Santa Fe, New Mexico

farther apart were the towns. I caught my first glimpse of the desert as we descended the passage over the San Gabriel Mountains into the Mojave. It was not the vast sea of sand my older sister had told me to expect. Instead, we had entered a broad, dry expanse surrounded by distant mountains and inhabited by mesas, sagebrush, and mysterious rock formations. Although I was generally a very talkative child, the desert was eerily quiet, and I was reluctant to break its silence. I sat soundlessly in my seat, looking out the window, simply staring at the scenery.

My aunt was waiting for us as we parked in front of the post office in Needles. I stepped out of the car, ducking behind my father, suddenly very shy. Cautiously peering around his leg, I saw a small woman, well under five feet in height. She had a friendly smile and was not at all the frightening person I had imagined. As I moved to my father's side, she bent down and quietly said, "It must be very hard to be so sick and then have to leave your family to live with relatives you don't know. I think *I* would find it a little scary. Are you a bit scared, Leila?"

"Mmm hmm," I whispered, biting my lip, but her gentle voice had somehow relieved a little of my fear. By the time the three of us had finished our early dinner, and Aunt Julie had ordered a huge serving of chocolate ice cream for me, I was pretty sure everything would be okay. As we left the diner, my father kissed me good-bye and then prepared for his long trip back to Los Angeles. Aunt Julie bundled me into her car. We crossed the bridge over the Colorado River and entered the state of Arizona. My life in California was suddenly behind me.

I sat quietly in the passenger seat, periodically sneaking glances at my aunt, this relative stranger with whom I would be living for the foreseeable future. Although I was still both nervous and excited, I didn't have time to dwell on either feeling. I was very tired after my long day, and soon my eyelids became heavy. I drifted off into a dreamless sleep. Aunt Julie, however, stayed awake late into the night, driving until we reached a hotel in Flagstaff.

The next day my aunt did her best to make me feel comfortable as we traveled the remaining three hundred miles to Santa Fe. She described life in Seton Village and told me about some of the things I would learn or be able to do. She would teach me the names of plants that grew in New Mexico, showing me how to press some of the glorious wildflowers that bloomed in the spring. My uncle would introduce me to the wildlife of the region—coyotes, wolves and prairie dogs, hawks, eagles, and roadrunners. He would even show me how to read the tracks some of those animals left behind. I found out that during the summer I would be allowed to attend Childervil, one of the camps she and my uncle ran, where I'd spend my days hiking, doing arts and crafts, going on field trips, and attending evening campfire councils with other children. I was very excited when I learned there were horses in the village, especially when Aunt Julie promised that one of the ranch hands would teach me to ride.

"And your uncle is an extraordinary storyteller," she informed me. "He will tell you many of the wonderful tales he has written about animals like Lobo, Bannertail, and Raggylug, Krag, Johnny Bear, and Silverspot. Having you in Santa Fe will be a wonderful adventure for all of us!"

When we arrived at the Castle, it was after midnight and I was still asleep. Someone must have carried me to my room because my next memory was of brilliant morning sunlight streaming through my window and the sound of muted voices in the distance. I sat up and looked around, momentarily confused by my surroundings. Shaking my head and thinking very hard, I finally realized I was in my new home in New Mexico.

As the low murmuring continued, I slid into slippers, pulled on a bathrobe, and tiptoed toward the source of the sound. Arriving at the end of a hallway, I opened the door to what I later found out was my aunt and uncle's study and discovered a very tall man talking to Aunt Julie. With long, tousled hair and a big mustache, he towered over my tiny aunt. Much to my surprise, he turned toward me, bent down, and scooped me up in his arms. "So," he said softly, "you must be little Leila come to live with us for a while. Welcome! Your aunt and I are very happy to have you here."

Even though I thought this giant with the white hair and very large hands was my uncle, I blurted out, "Are you my uncle? You look like a grandfather!"

"Yes, I am indeed your uncle," he replied, "but I suppose I do look rather like a grandfather. Most people call me Chief, but if you like, you can call me Granddaddy. It can be *our* special name."

From that moment on, Granddaddy he was. My nervousness had vanished, as if by magic.

Leila with Granddaddy

CHAPTER 2

Lots of "Oldest" in Santa Fe

"Look at all the snow!" I exclaimed. I was still surprised to see snow on the ground. It didn't snow in Los Angeles.

Granddaddy, Aunt Julie, and I were on our way into town from Seton Village. "Many people don't realize that it snows in Santa Fe," Granddaddy said. "They think Santa Fe is part of a dry, barren desert. It's actually located more than a mile above sea level, so we do get some winter snow. In fact, it snowed very hard the day before you arrived."

La Fonda, Santa Fe

Aunt Julie and Granddaddy were taking me out for a special welcome treat—lunch at a fancy hotel called La Fonda. As we parked the car, Granddaddy explained that there had been an inn on this corner of the Santa Fe Plaza for more than three hundred years. "La Fonda actually means 'the inn,'" he said. "This one is run by a man named Fred Harvey. He's a *very* good businessman! He's set up restaurants along the almost 2,000 miles of the Atchison, Topeka and Santa Fe Railway lines—all the way from St. Louis, Missouri, to San Francisco, California. Because of Mr. Harvey, train travelers can get good meals at every stop they make.

"We're going to have an excellent meal today," he promised. And indeed we did!

Chapel of San Miguel, the oldest U.S. church structure

Over lunch, Granddaddy told me that Santa Fe was known for being "the oldest"—the oldest capital city in the United States and the US city with the oldest house, oldest church structure, and oldest government building. "How old is oldest?" I asked.

"Well," said Granddaddy, "Santa Fe was here before the Pilgrims sailed on the Mayflower."

"I learned about the Pilgrims in school," I said. "They lived a really long time ago. Santa Fe must be very old."

As we left La Fonda, Aunt Julie pointed to the bustling public square in front of us and, sounding just like my first-grade teacher, said, "This square is very famous. It's known as the Plaza. A hundred years ago, it was the end of the Santa Fe Trail. Traders would start far away in Missouri, loading their covered wagons with manufactured goods from the North. Then they'd travel more than a thousand miles on the trail to Santa Fe, trading for gold and silver and horses and furs. It took eight or nine weeks, and the trail was dangerous. There were storms and bandits and rattlesnakes."

Santa Fe Trail

"Uggghhhh . . . I don't like snakes! I think I would have just stayed in Missouri!"

Walking through the Plaza, I noticed a long building on the far side. "Look at all those people sitting on the porch over there!" I shouted. "Who are they? Is that a famous building too? Why are there so many people here? Is this a park?"

"Hold on!" Granddaddy replied. "We'll answer every one of your questions, but let's go at them one at a time! Yes, the Plaza is kind of a park. It's the center of town. People meet friends here, sell things at markets, and sometimes just sit in the sun. That long, low building is the Palace of Governors and—"

"It's a palace?" I asked excitedly. "A real palace? Do a king and queen live in it?"

Pueblo Indians selling pottery and jewelry

The Blanket Weaver — Navajo

"Not exactly," Granddaddy explained. "It's where the governors who were in charge of Santa Fe and all the land in the territory used to live. Through the years, more than a hundred governors lived there. No one lives there now, but the building is still used as a museum. It's a very famous building because it's the oldest continuously used public building in the entire United States."

"Santa Fe certainly has a lot of *oldest* things," I said. I looked around. "Why *are* all those people sitting on the porch?" I asked.

"They're Indian artists and craftsmen from local communities," Aunt Julie explained. "For countless years they've been coming here to sell their handmade goods under the wooden beams—or *vigas*, as they're called—of that building. Shall we go take a look?"

Spread out on the porch were brightly colored blankets, many of them Navajo, with patterns that included stripes, diamonds, and other geometrics. "The Navajo tell the story of how a Spider Man taught them to make tools out of turquoise, white shell, abalone, and jet. He also created the first weaving loom using sunshine, lightning, and rain. When the loom was completed, a Spider Woman taught the Navajo how to weave. Their weaving is beautiful, isn't it?"

There were necklaces, bracelets, and rings displayed on several of the blankets, many made of silver and turquoise. Native American potters exhibited clay pots, bowls, and sculptures. A few craftsmen were even selling ceremonial drums made of stretched hide and wood. Lots of people were looking at the displays, and some were purchasing treasures to take home. I didn't have any money, so all I could do was look. But that was okay. When I went home, I drew colored pictures of some of the jewelry, cut my drawings out, and pasted them together to form my own necklaces and bracelets, which I wore for days.

That was the day I learned about adobe, too, when Aunt Julie informed me that the Palace of Governors and a number of other buildings in Santa Fe were made of wood and adobe. "Adobe," she explained, "is a mixture made mostly of dirt and clay and water. It gets very hard when it dries in the sun. The main reason it's used for buildings and houses in New Mexico is because it takes a very long time for it to get hot and then just as long for it to cool down, which keeps homes cool during hot summer days and warm during the cooler winter nights. Would *you* like to try making adobe bricks?"

"Yes, yes!" I cried enthusiastically. "Can we do it tomorrow?"

I had a wonderful first visit to Santa Fe, a city I came to know and love—and Aunt Julie and I did make adobe bricks the next day while I wore the paper turquoise necklace I created after arriving home.

Pueblo Indians selling pottery and jewelry

CHAPTER 3

How I Came to Be Called "Chipmunk"

I quickly adjusted to the routines of Seton Village. Most mornings, Maria, our housekeeper, would make me a breakfast of corn cakes with homemade prickly pear jelly. Then I would go outside and walk around the house, saying hello to the people who worked in the village. After I learned to ride, Aunt Julie and Granddaddy gave me a small horse named Molly. On days when he was not too busy, Ted, the man in charge of the horses, would saddle Molly for me, and I would ride all over the village. One day, after I had taken my morning ride, I was sitting on the front porch when a small animal skittered up next to me. I sat very still as it ran across my lap. A ranch hand who was working nearby told me it was a chipmunk and very quietly handed me some nuts to feed it. The chipmunk was munching on one of the nuts when Granddaddy and Aunt Julie came out onto the porch.

"May I take it to my room?" I whispered.

"For a little while," replied Granddaddy, "but we'll have to let it go later today."

I ran to my room and played with my chipmunk until Maria called me for lunch. Afterwards, when I returned to my room to take a nap, I had forgotten all about the chipmunk. I sat down on the bed to take off my shoes and heard a terrible screech. I felt something squirming underneath me and remembered my new pet. I screamed and burst into tears. Granddaddy came running to see what was wrong. Between sobs, I was finally able to tell him what had happened.

Granddaddy carefully lifted the bed covers. There, curled into a tiny ball, was the chipmunk, shaking with fear. Granddaddy picked up the frightened animal and placed it into the palm of his hand, petting it gently with his other hand. He walked outside with what I had hoped would be my pet and released it onto the ground with best wishes for a long life.

I had followed Granddady outside. He led me to the doorway and sat down on the stoop, patting the spot next to him to indicate where I should sit. "I know," he said, "that you really wanted the chipmunk as a pet, but wild animals are meant to be free. They have homes and families just like we do, and we need to respect that. Can we make a pact that from now on we'll watch wild animals where they belong—in their burrows or in the bushes?"

I nodded in agreement. Granddaddy went to fetch some paper and a pencil from his library. When he returned he drew a series of pictures showing the adventures of my chipmunk.

Chipmunks for Life, 1892

After that, Granddaddy often called me Chipmunk or referred to me as "the Chipmunk."

CHAPTER 4

Granddaddy's Stories

Portrait of Ernest Thompson Seton, 1906

Granddaddy was, as Aunt Julie had told me, an amazing storyteller. Almost every day I heard stories about wolves and rams, squirrels and bears, foxes, crows, rabbits, and even feral cats. Granddaddy told me that those adventures of Lobo, Silverspot, Bannertail, Slum Cat, Krag, Badlands Billy, and Johnny Bear were *true* and were about animals he had known. He wanted children to realize that animals, just like people, have intelligence and "heart." They loved their mates, protected their children, cared about their friends, were trustworthy and loyal, showed courage and fear, and were resourceful. Many of Granddaddy's stories were published in *Animal Heroes*, in *Lives of the Hunted*, and in his most famous book, *Wild Animals I Have Known*, a book that has remained in print since it was first published in 1898. I loved each and every one of the stories Granddaddy told me and, over time, the heroes of those tales became my friends.

CHAPTER 5

"Raggylug, the Story of a Cottontail Rabbit"

Story excerpted with slight adaptations from
Wild Animals I Have Known by Ernest Thompson Seton

One night after dinner, we were sitting by the fire when Granddaddy pulled me onto his lap and said, "Since you love rabbits, Chipmunk, I'm going to tell you the story of a cottontail rabbit named Raggylug."

Raggylug was a young cottontail rabbit. He lived in Old Olifant's Swamp with his mother, Molly Cottontail. A rabbit has many enemies—dogs, cats, foxes, hawks, owls, men, and even other rabbits. Molly knew she must teach her son how to survive the dangers of the swamp. Each day she taught him lessons that would hopefully protect him from the perils he would face.

One day, when Rag was only three weeks old, Molly tucked him into a bed of tall swamp grass, warning him to "lay low and say nothing, whatever happens." Rag lay very still, but he could not sleep. He was wide awake, and his bright eyes were taking in that part of his little green world that was straight above. A bluejay and a red-squirrel, two notorious thieves, were loudly berating each other for stealing. A scarlet and black ladybug, serenely waving her knobbled feelers, took a long walk up one grassblade, down another, and across the nest and over Rag's face—and yet he never moved nor even winked.

After awhile he heard a strange rustling of the leaves in the near thicket. It was an odd, continuous sound, and though it went this way and that way and came nearer, there was no patter of the feet with it. Rag had lived his whole life in the Swamp and yet had never heard anything like this. Of course his curiosity was greatly aroused. His mother had cautioned him to lay low, but that was understood to be in case of danger, and this strange sound without footfalls could not be anything to fear.

The low rasping sound went past close at hand, then to the right, then back, and seemed going away. Rag felt he knew what he was about; he wasn't a baby; it was his duty to learn what it was. He slowly raised his roly-poly body on his short fluffy legs, lifted his little round head above the covering of his nest and peeped out into the woods. The sound had ceased as soon as he moved. He saw nothing, so took one step forward to a clear view, and instantly found himself face to face with an enormous Black Serpent.

"Mammy," he screamed in mortal terror as the monster darted at him. With all the strength of his tiny limbs, he tried to run. But in a flash, the Snake had him by one ear and whipped around him with his coils to gloat over the helpless little baby bunny he had secured for dinner.

"'Mammy, Mammy!' he screamed in mortal terror."

"Mam-my—Mam-my," gasped poor little Raggylug as the cruel monster began slowly choking him to death. Very soon the little one's cry would have ceased, but bounding through the woods, straight as an arrow, came Mammy. No longer a shy, helpless little Molly Cottontail ready to fly from a shadow: the mother's love was strong in her. The cry of her baby had filled her with the courage of a hero, and—hop, she went over that horrible reptile. Whack, she struck down at him with her sharp hind claws as she passed, giving him such a stinging blow that he squirmed with pain and hissed with anger.

"M-a-m-m-y," came feebly from the little one. And Mammy came leaping again and again and again and struck harder and fiercer until the loathsome reptile let go the little *one's ear and tried to bite the old one as she leaped over. But all he got was a mouthful of wool each time, and Molly's fierce blows began to tell, as long bloody rips were torn in the Black Snake's scaly armor.*

Things were now looking bad for the Snake, and bracing himself for the next charge, he lost his tight hold on Baby Bunny, who at once wriggled out of the coils and away into the underbrush, breathless and terribly frightened, but unhurt, save that his left ear was much torn by the teeth of that dreadful Serpent.

Molly had now gained all she wanted. She had no notion of fighting for glory or revenge. Away she went into the woods and the little one followed the shining beacon of her snow-white tail until she led him to the safe corner of the swamp.

Throughout the telling, Granddaddy would periodically stop, pick up the pad of paper and the pencil that were always nearby, and draw pictures for me. That night I went back to my room with a number of treasures: drawings of Raggylug watching the world above from his bed of swamp grass, Molly Cottontail leaping at the snake as it held on to Raggylug's ear, and Molly and Rag nestled in a safer spot in Old Olifant's Swamp.

CHAPTER 6

Evening Drives

The Sangre de Cristo Mountains at sunset

Piñon tree at Seton Village

When we were not traveling, we usually went for a drive after dinner. No matter where we went, it was always Aunt Julie who drove. Granddaddy would sit in the front, and I would have the whole backseat to myself. My aunt would take us to different parts of Seton Village and the area surrounding Santa Fe, especially to places where we could see beautiful views of the Sangre de Cristo Mountains.

On one of our first drives, Granddaddy said, "Look carefully at the mountains, Chipmunk. They are as red as blood, aren't they? At sunset they often look like this. That's why they're called the Sangre de Cristo Mountains. It means 'Blood of Christ' in Spanish. The Sangre de Cristo are part of a much bigger chain of mountains called the Rocky Mountains. In California, you have the Sierra. In New Mexico, we have the Rockies. Aren't they beautiful?"

We would often stop during our drives. Granddaddy would point out animals and tell me about them. Sometimes he would sketch them. I loved it when I would spot a rabbit or an owl or a deer before Granddaddy did. He would laugh and tell me what a wonderful naturalist I was becoming. When we arrived home, he would weave delightful stories about the wildlife we had seen, often making sure my favorites—the cottontail rabbits—had a role in the tale.

Aunt Julie was an expert on the plant life of the Southwest. She would tell me about the trees and teach me the names of all the flowers. I also learned about cacti, including which ones were edible.

On one of our earliest trips into Santa Fe, Aunt Julie had stopped the car next to a lone tree. "This tree," she said, "is New Mexico's state tree, the piñon. Its nuts are delicious. Next autumn we'll try to gather some before the birds get to them. This is the tree that produces that wonderful odor you keep calling your 'Santa Fe smell.' Piñon logs are what many people here burn in their fireplaces when it's cold."

This aroma permeated the Santa Fe air throughout the winter season. I can, to this day, close my eyes and remember the sweet scent. It immediately transports me back to those magical days in New Mexico.

Sometimes Aunt Julie and I would pick wildflowers. I would take them home and press and label them.

How Aunt Julie Pressed Wildflowers

1. Select a flower that is dry.
2. Place the flower on a piece of white paper, laying the leaves and petals flat.
3. Put another piece of white paper on top of the flower.
4. Sandwich the wildflower and paper between two pieces of cardboard or heavy paper.
5. Place several very heavy books on top of the wildflower and leave it to dry for four or five days.
6. Remove the books and cardboard and leave the flower in a dry, airy space for another week or two.
7. After it is thoroughly dry, you can place it in a scrapbook, glue it on special paper and frame it to create a wall hanging, or use it to decorate a greeting card.

The prickly pear, which tastes a little bit like watermelon, is one of the edible kinds of cacti that grows in New Mexico. People use its fruit in cookies, jams, meat dishes, breads, and other foods. Maria, our housekeeper, often made salad dressing with prickly pears. She would mash them and press the pulp through a sieve. Then she would add oil and vinegar, salt and pepper, and some spices. I *loved* Maria's special dressing.

Santa Fe Phlox

Dakota Vervain

Hairy Golden Aster

Buffalo Gourd

Banana Yucca

Claret Cup Cactus

Wildflowers and cacti found at and near Seton Village

CHAPTER 7

Trailing

Many years before I arrived in Santa Fe, Granddaddy founded the League of Woodcraft Indians. Woodcraft was about the outdoor life and incorporated many Native American traditions. Boys camped out, put up teepees, learned Indian and nature crafts, played games, fished, and in general spent lots of time learning about and enjoying the wonders of nature. They were taught to lead healthy lives, to abide by a code of honor, to live simply, and to respect and care for our natural world. In *The Book of Woodcraft* and *The Birch Bark Roll*, Granddaddy described the skills boys would need to acquire. He also wrote *Two Little Savages*, a novel about two boys living by the code of the Woodcraft Indians.

Granddaddy traveled to England in the early 1900s and shared his ideas about the Woodcraft League with British General Robert Baden-Powell. They, along with several others, including Daniel Beard, helped found the Boy Scouts of America. Although Granddaddy served as the first Chief of the Boy Scouts, he later re-established the Woodcraft League.

While I lived in Santa Fe, Granddaddy taught me many of the Woodcraft League skills, including those needed for trailing—the art of wildlife tracking. I learned to be a detective of sorts and, after I became familiar with the paths around Seton Village, spent many hours trying to discover which animal had left each set of tracks I came across, what the animal was doing, where it was headed, and sometimes, if I discovered scat, what it had eaten. I would often imitate Granddaddy and try to sketch the tracks. I was never very good at drawing them, but Granddaddy gave me sketches he had made and, in time, I could identify the tracks of a number of different animals and follow the tracks to their end.

"One of the things you need to remember, Chipmunk, is that no two animals leave the same track. Now it would be best for me to show you this after it has just snowed." So my lessons began in the winter, after one of our snowfalls. "This is a wonderfully rewarding way of learning the methods and life of an animal. The trail records with perfect truthfulness everything that it did or tried to do," Granddaddy told me.

Granddaddy taught me that the easiest tracks to find were those made by cats and dogs. "See how round the toe pads of a cat are? That is because their paws are so soft. Do you know why there are no claw marks?"

"I do! I do!" I exclaimed. "It's because cats can pull their claws in. That's what our ranch hand's cat does all the time when she sits on my lap."

"You're right, Chipmunk," said Granddaddy. "It's called retractability. Now look at this. The feet are equal in length—"

"But the front feet are fatter," I cried.

"Right you are! Can you see how the tracks look like the cat is only moving on two feet? It's because the cat puts its rear feet exactly where its front feet stepped. The cat does this perfectly, so it is silent when it walks. This makes the cat a great hunter."

"What are these?" I asked, pointing to a set of tracks. "They're not neat like a cat's. What are all these lines in front and behind the tracks?"

Seton drawing of cat and dog tracks

"Those are dog prints. They were probably made by our cook's dog," he answered. "The lines are from its claws because a dog's claws are not—"

"—retractable!" I exclaimed.

"That's correct, Chipmunk. What else do you notice?"

I studied the tracks in the snow. "His rear feet don't step where the front feet do," I said.

"Chipmunk, you are learning to be an excellent tracker!"

I may never have become an *excellent* tracker, but in time I became a fairly proficient one, and I spent many hours pursuing this pastime, learning about the habits of a variety of wild animals.

Seton drawing of animal tracks

CHAPTER 8

"The Cat and the Skunk"

Story excerpted from *Two Little Savages* by Ernest Thompson Seton

Two Little Savages is a book about the adventures of Yan, a character Granddaddy modeled on himself. It remains one of his most beloved books. Yan is a young boy from town who loves wildlife and all things related to Native Americans. When he becomes ill and does not recover completely, his doctor recommends sending him to a farm for a year. So Yan is sent to live with Mr. and Mrs. Raften and their son Sam. (This sounds a little like what happened to me, doesn't it?) Together, the boys begin an adventure in the woods, building their own teepee, learning the names and uses of native plants, acquiring knowledge about the birds and animals found in the area—even how to identify their tracks—and playing Indian games. I love the story of "The Cat and the Skunk" in *Two Little Savages* because it reminds me of when I learned about animal tracks—and because the story is so vividly told that every time I read it, I can almost smell the skunk spray and feel it burning my eyes!

Mud-turtle tracks

Yan now turned down the creek to the lower mud album and was puzzled by a new track like this. He sketched it, but before the drawing was done, it dawned on him that this must be the track of a young Mud-turtle. He also saw a lot of very familiar tracks, not a few being those of the common Cat, and he wondered why they should be about so much and yet so rarely seen. He lay down on his breast at the edge of the brook, which had been cut in the channel with steep clay walls six feet high and twenty feet apart. The stream was very small now—a mere thread of water zigzagging over the level muddy floor of the "cañon," as Yan loved to call it. A broad, muddy margin at each side of the water made a fine place of record for the traveling Four-foots, and tracks new and old were there in abundance.

As he lay there thinking, a slight movement nearer the creek caught his eye. A large Basswood had been blown down. Like most of its kind, it was hollow. Its trunk was buried in the tangle of the rank summer growth, but a branch had been broken off and left a hole in the main stem. In the black cavern of the hole there appeared a head with shining green eyes; then out there glided onto the log a common gray Cat. She sat there in the sunshine, licked her paws, dressed her fur generally, stretched her claws and legs after the manner of her kind, walked to the end of the log, then down the easy slope to the bottom of the cañon.

Here she took a drink, daintily shook the water from her paws, and set the hair just right with a stroke. Then to Yan's amazement, she examined all the tracks, much as he had done, though it seemed clear that her nose, not her eyes, was judge. She walked up and down stream, leaving some very fine impressions that Yan mentally resolved to have in his notebook very soon, suddenly stopped, looked upward and around, a living picture of elegance, sleekness and grace, with eyes of green fire, then deliberately leaped from the creek bed to the tangle of the bank and disappeared.

This was a very commonplace happening, but the fact of a house Cat taking to the woods lent her unusual interest, and Yan felt much of the thrill that a truly wild animal would have given him and had gone far enough in art to find exquisite pleasure in the series of pictures the Cat had presented to his eyes.

He lay there for some minutes expecting her to reappear; then far up the creek, he heard slight rattling of the gravel. He turned and saw not the Cat but a very different and somewhat larger animal. Low, thick-set, jet black, with white marks and an immense bushy tail—Yan recognized the Skunk at once, although he had never before met a wild one in daylight. It came at a deliberate waddle, nosing this way and that. It rounded the bend and was nearly opposite Yan, when three little Skunks of this year's brood came toddling after the mother.

The old one examined the tracks much as the Cat had done, and Yan got a singular sense of brotherhood in seeing the wild things at his own study.

Then the old Skunk came to the fresh tracks of the Cat and paused so long to smell them that the three young ones came up and joined in. One of the young ones went to the bank where the Cat came down. As it blew its little nose over the fresh scent, the old Skunk waddled to the place, became quite interested, then climbed the bank. The little ones followed in a disjointed procession, varied by one of them tumbling backward from the steep trail.

The old Skunk reached the top of the bank, then mounted the log and followed unerringly the Cat's back trail to the hole in the trunk. Down this she peered a minute, then, sniffing, walked in, till nothing could be seen but her tail. Now Yan heard loud, shrill mewing from the log, "Mew, mew, m-e-u-w, m-e-e-u-w," and the old Skunk came backing out holding a small gray Kitten.

The little thing mewed and spit energetically, holding on to the inside of the log. But the old Skunk was too strong—she dragged it out. Then holding it down with both paws, she got a good firm grip of its neck and turned to carry it down to the bed of the brook. The Kitten struggled vigorously, and at last got its claws into the Skunk's eye and gave such a wrench that the ill-smelling villain loosened its hold a little and so gave the Kitten another chance to squeal, which it did with a will, putting all its strength into a succession of heartrending mee-ow—mee-ows. Yan's heart was touched. He was about to dash to the rescue when there was a scrambling in the far grass, a rush of gray, and the Cat—the old mother Cat was on the scene, a picture of demon rage, eyes ablaze, fur erect, ears back. With the spring of a Deer and the courage of a Lion she made for the black murderer. Eye could not follow the flashings of her paws. The Skunk recoiled and stared stupidly, but not for long; nothing was "long" about it. Her every superb muscle was tingling with force and mad with hate as the mother Cat closed like a swooping Falcon. The Skunk had no time to aim that dreadful gun, and in the excitement fired a volley of the deadly musky spray backward, drenching her own young as they huddled in the trail.

Tooth and claw and deadly grip—the old Cat raged and tore, the black fur flew in every direction, and the Skunk for once lost her head and fired random shots of choking spray that drenched herself as well as the Cat. The Skunk's head and neck were terribly torn. The air was suffocating with the poisonous musk. The Skunk was desperately wounded and threw herself backward into the water. Blinded and choking, though scarcely bleeding, the old Cat would have followed even there, but the Kitten, wedged under the log, mewed piteously and stayed the mother's fury. She dragged it out unharmed but drenched with musk and carried it quickly to the den in the hollow log, then came out again and stood erect, blinking her blazing eyes—for they were burning with the spray—lashing her tail, the image of a Tigress eager to fight either part or all the world for the little ones she nursed. But the old Skunk had had more than enough. She scrambled off down the cañon. Her three young ones had tumbled over each other to get out of the way when they got that first accidental charge of their mother's battery. She waddled away, leaving a trail of blood and smell, and they waddled after, leaving an odor just as strong.

Yan was thrilled by the desperate fight of the heroic old Cat. Her whole race went up higher in his esteem that day; and the fact that the house Cat really could take to the woods and there maintain herself by hunting was all that was needed to give her a place in his list of animal heroes.

At length all danger of attack seemed over, and Pussy, shaking her paws and wiping her eyes, glided into her hole. Oh, what a shock it must have been to the poor Kittens, though partly prepared by their brother's unsavory coming back. There was the mother, whose return had always been heralded by a delicious odour of fresh Mouse or bird, interwoven with a loving and friendly odour of Cat that was in itself a promise of happiness. Scent is the main thing in Cat life, and now the hole was darkened by a creature that was rank and every nasal guarantee of deadly enmity. Little wonder that they all fled, puffing and spitting to the darkest corners. It was a hard case; all the little stomachs were upset for a long time. They could do nothing but make the best of it and get used to it. The den never ceased to stink while they were there, and even after they grew up and lived elsewhere many storms passed overhead before the last of the Skunk smell left them.

" ...the old cat raged and tore..."

CHAPTER 9

A Porcupine Hunt

"Time to go, Chipmunk," Granddaddy called. "Tonight we are going on a porcupine hunt."

"What's a porkypine?" I asked as I climbed into the car. I loved our evening rides, and I knew this would be a great adventure, regardless of what a "porkypine" was.

Granddaddy drew me a picture of one and said it was pronounced *pork-you-pine*. As he created his drawing, he told me about this bristly animal. "It looks a little bit like its relative, the beaver, but it's a land animal. It moves verrrrry slowly and rather awkwardly. See how hairy it is," he said, pointing to the sketch. "Its front hair is pretty soft, but the hair on its back, sides, and tail is mixed with special spiky hairs called quills. A porcupine is a peaceful, solitary animal, but when it's scared, its quills stand up, and it looks like a pincushion." Granddaddy sketched a picture of a porcupine looking like a great big pincushion. It was funny and made me laugh.

"Sometimes," he continued, "a porcupine uses its quills to protect itself from other animals. Many people think porcupines *shoot* their quills, but they really don't do that." Granddaddy drew a picture of quills flying off a porcupine, and put an "X" through it. He then drew a series of pictures showing a dog that got too close to a porcupine. The porcupine turned and flailed its tail back and forth at the dog. The dog ended up with quills sticking out all over its face. Granddaddy wrote *"OUCH!"* underneath the pictures.

"Why are we going on a porcupine hunt?" I asked. "We might scare the porcupine, and then *we* will have quills sticking out all over our faces. It would *hurt!*"

"Don't worry, Chipmunk," Granddaddy assured me, "Aunt Julie and I will make sure you don't end up with porcupine quills sticking out of your body. And we're not really going to *capture* the porcupine, just some of its quills."

"As long as those quills aren't stuck in me," I murmured.

It was dusk as my aunt parked the car. Granddaddy had promised porcupines didn't shoot their quills and I would be safe, but I was still scared. We waited patiently near a grove of trees and soon a huge, prickly porcupine came snuffling by. Aunt Julie had a big blanket with her. She fearlessly leapt out at the porcupine and threw the blanket over it. The animal grunted and moaned. I could see it thrashing its tail under the blanket, back and forth, back and forth. It continued to shriek and grumble for what seemed like a very long time. When it

Porcupine tracks illustrating the tail drag print that is also left on the ground as the porcupine walks

finally calmed down, Granddaddy stepped closer, making soothing sounds while he gingerly pulled the blanket away from the bristly animal. I watched anxiously. Would the porcupine attack Granddaddy? Granddaddy stepped back, blanket in hand. The porcupine looked surprised as it sniffed the air. Then it clumsily waddled on its way towards the nearest tree.

There were porcupine quills stuck to the inside of the blanket. Granddaddy carefully rolled the blanket into another blanket and placed it in the car. I warily stepped into the backseat, curling myself into the corner as far away from the bundle of quills as possible. While Aunt Julie drove us back to the Castle, Granddaddy talked about quillworking, but I wasn't really listening. I was not convinced the quills wouldn't stick me if I accidentally got too close. When we arrived home, I jumped out of the car, anxious to get away from the prickly quills. Granddaddy lifted the blanket cautiously and placed it near the front porch.

The next morning, Aunt Julie put on gloves and gently extracted quills from the blanket. I sat on Granddaddy's lap watching her. "Do you think it hurt the porcupine when we took its quills?" I asked.

"You know I would never do anything to hurt a wild creature," he reminded me. "Porcupines have thousands and thousands of quills. When I was in Canada, I once counted the quills on a porcupine. There were 36,450 quills on just that one animal. We only gathered a couple hundred quills yesterday. In just a few months, the porcupine will grow new ones where the old ones were."

I was relieved—we hadn't injured the porcupine. I was only seven and couldn't count to anywhere near 36,000, but I knew it was a lot. We hadn't collected that many quills. Our porcupine would be okay.

Aunt Julie cleaned the quills and soaked them in soapy water to remove the oils. She did this several times until the quills were bright white. Then she laid them on paper to dry.

"Okay, Chipmunk," Aunt Julie said as we headed inside to the kitchen, "we're going to dye the quills." She placed big pots of water on the stove and added different plants to each one—wild sunflowers to get a bright yellow, squaw currant to get red, and indigo to get blue. "If we could find wild grapes, we could make black too," Aunt Julie added. "Now," she told me as she took the sugar out of the cabinet, "we're going to add the secret ingredient!"

"SUGAR? Is that the secret 'gredient?" I asked.

Seton moccasin designs

"Surprising, isn't it? I used to have so much trouble dying the quills," she replied, "even after cleaning the oils off of them with the soapy water." Then Aunt Julie explained to me how an old Indian woman told her to add sugar. "It seemed odd," Aunt Julie said, "but I tried it and it worked like magic!"

And it did. Our quills had such beautiful colors.

Granddaddy and I helped Aunt Julie spread the quills out after they were dyed so they could dry again. The next day we rubbed each quill with oil.

"Why did we take all the oil off the quills if we're just going to put it back on?" I asked.

"It does seem like a lot of extra work, doesn't it?" Aunt Julie said. "Well, first we rub the oil off the quills so the dye will soak in. Once the quills are dyed, we have to rub them with new oil to keep them from getting brittle and breaking. By doing this, we keep the quills strong so we can embroider with them."

Finally, the quills were ready to use. Aunt Julie embroidered a pair of moccasins, while Granddaddy helped me embroider a leather headband. First, we sketched a very simple design on a strip of leather. After that, we flattened the quills, dampened them, and began our stitching, attaching the quills using a needle and heavy thread. It took several days to complete the embroidery, but Granddaddy told me it was a good lesson in patience. As we worked on the headband, he told me several stories about Bannertail, a gray squirrel raised by a cat. I loved Bannertail and often begged Granddaddy to tell me more about the animal's adventures.

Later in the week, after I had listened to many stories, Granddaddy and I finished my headband by attaching feathers to it. It was so beautiful that I refused to take it off—even when I went to bed that night.

Seton painting of untitled warbonnet

CHAPTER 10

"The Foundling"

Chapter 1 of *Bannertail: The Story of a Gray Squirrel* by Ernest Thompson Seton

It was a rugged old tree standing sturdy and big among the slender second-growth. The woodmen had spared it because it was too gnarled and too difficult for them to handle. But the Woodpecker, and a host of wood-folk that look to the Woodpecker for lodgings, had marked and used it for many years. Its every cranny and borehole was inhabited by some quaint elfin of the woods; the biggest hollow of all, just below the first limb, had done duty for two families of the Flickers who first made it, and now was the homing hole of a mother Gray Squirrel.

Fluffing his Tail

She appeared to have no mate; at least none was seen. No doubt the outlaw gunners could have told a tale, had they cared to admit that they went gunning in springtime; and now the widow was doing the best she could by her family in the big gnarled tree. All went well for a while, then one day, in haste maybe, she broke an old rule in Squirreldom; she climbed her nesting tree openly, instead of going up its neighbor, and then crossing to the den by way of the overhead branches. The farm boy who saw it gave a little yelp of savage triumph; his caveman nature broke out. Clubs and stones were lying near; the whirling end of a stick picked off the mother Squirrel as she tried to escape with a little one in her mouth. Had he killed two dangerous enemies, the boy could not have yelled louder. Then up the tree he climbed and found in the nest two living young ones. With these in his pocket he descended. When on the ground he found that one was dead, crushed in climbing down. Thus only one little Squirrel was left alive, only one of the family that he had seen, the harmless mother and two helpless, harmless little ones dead in his hands.

Why? What good did it do him to destroy all this beautiful wild life? He did not know. He did not think of it at all. He had yielded only to the wild ancestral instinct to kill when came a chance to kill, for he must remember that instinct was implanted, wild animals were either terrible enemies or food that must be got at any price.

"His Kittenhood"

The excitement over, the boy looked at the helpless squirming thing in his hand, and a surge of remorse came on him. He could not feed it; it must die of hunger. He wished that he knew of some other nest into which he might put it. He drifted back to the barn. The mew of a young Kitten caught his ear. He went to the manger. Here was the old Cat with the one Kitten that had been left her of her brood born two days back. Remembrance of many Field-mice, Chipmunks, and some Squirrels killed by that old green-eyed huntress, struck a painful note. Yes! No matter what he did, the old Cat would surely get, kill, and eat the orphan Squirrel.

Then he yielded to a sudden impulse and said, "Here it is; eat it now." He dropped the little stranger into the nest beside the Kitten. The Cat turned toward it, smelled it suspiciously once or twice, then licked its back, picked it up in her mouth, and tucked it under her arm, where half an hour later, the boy found it taking dinner alongside its newfound foster-brother, while motherly old Cat leaned back with chin in the air, half-closed eyes, and purring the happy, contented purr of mother pride. Now, indeed, the future of the Foundling was assured.

CHAPTER 11

A Valuable Lesson

I was a curious little girl and the area around Seton Village gave me lots of room for exploration. Granddaddy would encourage me to wander about outside to discover the wonders of nature. The country was so very different from the city.

During one of my wanderings, I saw a beautiful blue bird almost hidden in the needles of a piñon tree. The bird flew off as I approached, but I was intent on finding out whether it had nested there. I climbed the small tree to take a closer look and was so excited when I saw a nest made of twigs, bark, and grasses. In the nest were four small pale blue eggs. Very carefully, I picked up one of the eggs, climbed down the tree, and ran into the house to show Granddaddy what I had found.

Before I found Granddaddy, I saw Maria, our housekeeper, and I decided to display my amazing discovery to her first. I hid the egg behind my back and told her to hold out her hand so that I could put a surprise in it. As I went to place the small egg into Maria's hand, it slipped from my fingers and fell to the floor, where it broke. I cried out and ran to tell Granddaddy.

"Where did you find the egg, Leila?" Granddaddy asked as he took my hand and walked me toward the window. I was scared. Granddaddy seldom called me Leila. He clearly seemed annoyed with me as I pointed to the tree. "Look at the bird flying around the tree. It's the mother Pinyon Jay. She knows one of her eggs is missing, and she is looking for it."

"I didn't mean for the egg to break," I said.

"I know that, Leila, but jays have many natural enemies, including squirrels and coyotes. They shouldn't have to worry about humans hurting their eggs." He let go of my hand and walked away.

I realized I had disappointed Granddaddy. That evening I told him I was very sorry for taking the egg and for making the mother bird sad.

"I know you did not mean to cause harm, Chipmunk, but you did. In the future, you need to be very careful and think before you act. Ask yourself if what you are doing could hurt another person or creature. You must try very hard not to do anything that is harmful to a living thing," Granddaddy said.

"I promise to try and think before I act," I replied. "I don't want to do anything that will harm any living creature."

I climbed onto Granddaddy's lap. He smiled at me and then hugged me tightly. "Let's have a story," he said. "Since we had a very serious talk about birds, I think I'll tell you a funny bird story." And so he told me about some chickadees who failed to heed the warning to fly south to a warmer climate for the winter and why, because of that, chickadees still go crazy once a year. Throughout the telling, Granddaddy drew captivating little pictures to show me what was happening. I laughed in delight at the plight of these birds and their cheerfulness in spite of the fact that they annually have to brave the harsh winter snows.

Seton drawing, *Untitled Row of Animals*

CHAPTER 12

"Why the Chickadee Goes Crazy Once a Year"

Story from *Lives of the Hunted* by Ernest Thompson Seton

A long time ago, when there was no winter in the north, the Chickadees lived merrily in the woods with their relatives, and cared for nothing but to get all the pleasure possible out of their daily life in the thickets. But at length Mother Carey [or Mother Nature, as we often call her today] *sent them all a warning that they must move to the south, for hard frost and snow were coming on their domains, with starvation close behind.*

The Nuthatches and other cousins of the Chickadees took this warning seriously, and set about learning how and when to go; but Tomtit, who led his brothers, only laughed and turned a dozen wheels around a twig that served him for a trapeze.

"Go to the south?" said he. "Not I; I am too well contented here; and as for frost and snow, I never saw any and have no faith in them."

But the Nuthatches and Kinglets were in such a state of bustle that at length the Chickadees did catch a little of the excitement, and left off play for a while to question their friends; and they were not pleased with what they learned, for it seemed that all of them were to make a journey that would last many days, and the little Kinglets were actually going as far as the Gulf of Mexico. Besides, they were to fly by night in order to avoid their enemies the Hawks, and the weather at this season was sure to be stormy. So the Chickadees said it was all nonsense, and went off in a band, singing and chasing one another through the woods.

But their cousins were in earnest. They bustled about, making their preparations and learned beforehand what it was necessary for them to know about the way. The great wide river running southward, the moon at height, and the trumpeting of the Geese were to be their guides, and they were to sing as they flew in the darkness, to keep from being scattered.

The noisy, rollicking Chickadees were noisier than ever as the preparations went on, and made sport of their relatives, who were now gathered in great numbers in the woods along the river, and at length, when the proper time of the moon came, the cousins arose in a body and flew away in gloom. The Chickadees said that the cousins all were crazy, made some good jokes about the Gulf of Mexico, and then dashed away in a game of tag through the woods, which, by the by, seemed rather deserted now, while the weather, too, was certainly turning cool.

At length the frost and snow really did come, and the Chickadees were in a woeful case. Indeed, they were frightened out of their wits, and dashed hither and thither, seeking in vain for someone to set them aright on the way to the south. They flew wildly about the woods, till they were truly crazy. I suppose there was not a Squirrel-hole or a hollow log in the neighborhood that some Chickadee did not enter to inquire if this was the Gulf of Mexico. But no one could tell anything about it, no one was going that way, and the great river was hidden under ice and snow.

About this time a messenger from Mother Carey was passing with a message to the Caribou in the far north; but all he could tell the Chickadees was that he could not be their guide, as he had no instructions, and, at any rate, he was going the other way. Besides, he told them, they had had the same notice as their cousins, whom they had called "crazy"; and from what he knew of Mother Carey, they would probably have to brave it out here all through the snow, not only now, but in all following winters, so they might as well make the best of it.

This was sad news for the Tomtits, but they were brave little fellows, and seeing they could not help themselves, they set about making the best of it. Before a week had gone by, they were in their usual good spirits again, scrambling about the twigs or chasing one another as before. They had still the assurance that winter would end. So filled were they with this idea that even at its commencement, when a fresh blizzard came on, they would gleefully remark to one another that it was a "sign of spring," and one or another of the band would lift his voice in the sweet little chant that we all know so well: "spring soon." Another would take it up and re-echo: "spring coming," and they would answer and repeat the song until the dreary woods rang again with the good news, and the people learned to love the brave little Bird that sets his face so cheerfully to meet so hard a case.

But to this day, when the chill wind blows through the deserted woods, the Chickadees seem to lose their wits for a few days, and dart into all sorts of odd and dangerous places. They may then be found in great cities, or open prairies, cellars, chimneys, and hollow logs; and the next time you find one of the wanderers in any such place, be sure to remember that Tomtit goes crazy once a year, and probably went into his strange retreat in search of the Gulf of Mexico.

CHAPTER 13

The College of Indian Wisdom

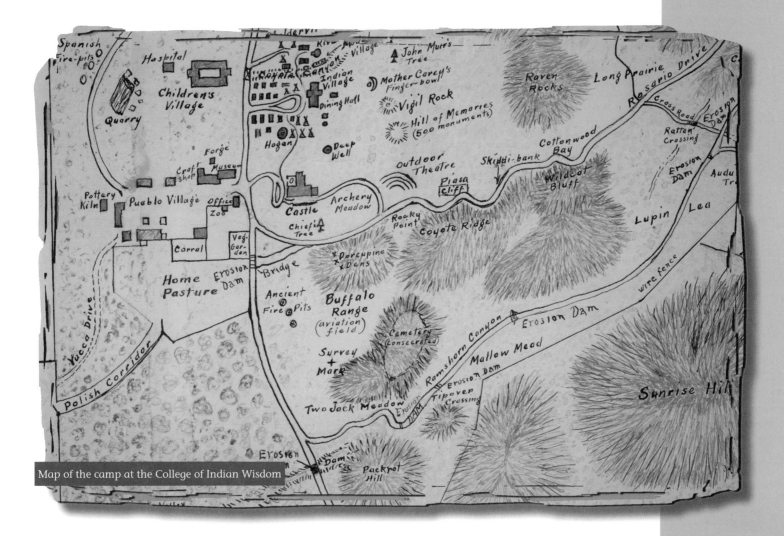

Map of the camp at the College of Indian Wisdom

Leila at summer camp, 1933

Aunt Julie in lecture costume, 1935

Each summer Aunt Julie and Granddaddy ran the Seton Institute, part of Seton College of Indian Wisdom. There were three different camps—one for adults, one for thirteen- to seventeen-year-olds, and Childervil, the camp for six- to twelve-year-olds. I, of course, attended Childervil where I learned all about the Woodcraft League. Granddaddy was "the Chief" during the summer sessions and everyone, including me, called him that while the camp was going on.

During the camps, I continued to live with Aunt Julie and the Chief in the Castle. Other campers, however, stayed in teepees, boxcars, cabins, the longhouse, and the other small buildings at Seton Village. Native American artisans and experts in arts and crafts, nature, music, dance, and folklore traveled to Santa Fe from all over the country to teach us. We learned Native American songs and how to make rattles and drums. We put on plays about Indian history and "Granddaddy's animals." We experienced the magic of the campfire. We attended nature classes where we studied about local trees, flowers, birds, and animals. We made our own arrows and used them with our bows during archery classes. We took horseback rides and nature hikes. We even did some mountain climbing. My favorite classes were the arts and crafts ones in which we learned to make Indian costumes, headdresses, and moccasins and studied Navajo weaving, pottery, beading, basketry, and woodcarving.

Among the most useful classes at camp were the ones about sign language and picture writing. "What is sign language?" I asked Granddaddy when he had introduced the subject to me, several months before my first summer camp experience.

"Well, Chipmunk, it's a simple method of asking questions and giving answers without using your voice—that is, a way of talking with your hands. It is used by all the Plains Indians and by thousands of other people throughout the world. Think about this. Does a policeman on a crowded street use sign language?"

"I don't think so," I replied. "No one would know what he was trying to say."

"Is that really true? What does the officer do when he wishes to stop all cars?"

"He puts his hand up like this," I said, holding my hand up flat with the palm forward.

"Exactly!" Granddaddy said. "That's sign language, and that's the way I sometimes talk when I meet with Indian chiefs. One of the best sign talkers I ever met was the Crow Indian, White Swan, who had been one of the scouts for United States Army General George Armstrong Custer. In a very famous battle, the Battle of Little Bighorn, White Swan was badly wounded and left for dead. He escaped, but afterwards he could neither speak nor hear. Because sign talk was familiar to the Crow people, he was able to use it to communicate. He and I became good friends, and I took many sign language lessons from him. White Swan was the person who inspired me to seriously study the language."

"When would *I* use it, Granddaddy?" I asked.

"Well, you could use it when you were somewhere very noisy or if you wanted to tell someone something that you didn't want anyone else to understand. You could also use it anywhere where you are not allowed to speak aloud—like in school or at a concert or in a library. Of course, there are times it won't work. It's useless in the dark, and it will not serve on the telephone! Nevertheless, it is a good language to learn." Granddaddy taught me many signs that he and I sometimes used in place of voices.

Hand Signs

Yes – a head nod

No – a shake of the head

You – point at the person

Me – point at yourself

Go – move hand forward, palm first

Come – draw hand toward oneself, palm first

Stop – one hand raised, flat, palm forward

Silence – forefinger across lips

Listen – flat hand behind ear

Friendship – hands clasped

Sleep – Lay the right cheek on the right flat hand

Up – forefinger pointed and moved upward

Down – forefinger pointed and moved downward

Eat – Throw the flat hand several times past the mouth in a curve

Drink – Hold the right hand as though holding a cup near the mouth and tip it up

You can find many more signs in Granddaddy's *The Book of Woodcraft* or in his sign language dictionary, *Sign Talk: A Universal Signal Code.*

Although I found sign language a little challenging because I was such a talkative child, I used it sometimes. What I really loved, however, was the picture writing that we learned at camp. Granddaddy told us it was also called pictography or ideography because the pictures represent *ideas,* not words or letters. "For example," he explained, "each chief, warrior, and scout has a totem, a drawing that stands for his name or for himself. A man's name is expressed by his totem. Thus, the following means, *"Today, 20th Sun Thunder Moon. After three days, 'Deerfoot,' Chief of the Flying Eagles, comes to our Standing Rock Camp."*

"Pictographs can serve as an important way to record history, too," Granddaddy told us. He then took us up to the Castle where he showed us something amazing: pictographs created by White Swan illustrating the Battle of Little Bighorn. He told us that these were among just a few drawings that still existed of what is often called "Custer's Last Stand," and he explained that he had purchased them during the time White Swan was giving him sign language lessons. For many years these pictographs decorated the walls of Seton Castle. In 1967, when my aunt donated the contents of Granddaddy's library to the Boy Scouts of America, these were part of the treasure-trove. If you ever travel to the Boy Scout camp in New Mexico, you can see them at the Philmont Museum and Seton Memorial Library.

Granddaddy drew many Indian pictographs in *The Book of Woodcraft,* and I spent hours copying them and writing him little notes using those pictographs. Here are some pictographs you can use to create your own notes or stories. You might even create some new symbols.

Symbol	Meaning	Symbol	Meaning	Symbol	Meaning
—	Level		Man		Good
→	Direction forward		Woman		Bad
←	Direction backward		Baby		Water
	Sun or day		Scout		Good water
	Sunrise		Scouting		Good water in 3 arrow flights
	Sunset	?	Question		One-night camp
	Noon	X	Yes		More permanent camp
	Night	O	No		Village
	Day back one, or yesterday		Doubtful		Town
	Day forward one, or to-morrow	or	Peace		Heap or many
	Moon, or month	or	War		I have found
	Rain		Surrender		Bear
	Snow		Prisoner		Grizzly bear
			Enemy		Chipmunk
			Friend		Dead bear
					Treaty of peace

Seton painting of Lobo

CHAPTER 14

"Lobo, the King of Currumpaw"

Story excerpted from *Wild Animals I have Known* by Ernest Thompson Seton

In the evenings, the Chief would gather me and the other children attending camp around a council fire. Sometimes he would teach us about the stars. He would ask us to first find the Big Dipper. Then, with the Big Dipper as our compass point, he would help us locate other constellations, like Cassiopeia and Orion. Regardless of what else the Chief talked about at the campfire, he would always tell us stories until it was bedtime. After all the children except me returned to their cabins, the Chief would tell even more stories to the adults. Their campfire would go on late into the night. Because I lived in the Castle and not in the camp, I was allowed to stay with the adults. Often, at the beginning of a camp session, he would tell his most famous story, "Lobo, the King of Currumpaw."

Old Lobo, or the king, as the Mexicans called him, was the gigantic leader of a remarkable pack of gray wolves that had ravaged the Currumpaw Valley for a number of years. All the shepherds and ranchmen knew him well and wherever he appeared with his trusty band, terror reigned supreme among the cattle, and wrath and despair among their owners. Old Lobo was a giant among wolves, and was cunning and strong in proportion to his size. His voice at night was well known and easily distinguished from that of any of his fellows... When the deep roar of the old king came booming down the cañon, the watcher bestirred himself and prepared to learn in the morning that fresh and serious inroads had been made among the herds.

Through the years, many hunters had traveled to Currumpaw to try to earn the large reward the ranchers had promised to anyone who could rid the area of the wolves that were pillaging their ranch lands. Each, in his turn, had failed. Granddaddy went to New Mexico to hunt Lobo's pack in 1893. Lobo proved to be an intelligent and wily opponent, not easily captured. Although Granddaddy was often frustrated by Lobo's craftiness, he also came to greatly admire the wolf. Many times Granddaddy set traps for Lobo and just as many times, Lobo failed to fall prey to them. Once when Granddaddy had laid out poisoned meat for Lobo's pack, confident he was about to put an end to Lobo's raids on the cattle ranches, he again discovered that Lobo had evaded him.

The next morning I went forth, eager to know the result. I soon came on the fresh trail of the robbers, with Lobo in the lead—his track was always easily distinguished. An ordinary wolf's forefoot is 4½ inches long, that of a large wolf 4¾ inches, but Lobo's, as measured a number of times, was 5½ inches from claw to heel; I afterward found that his other proportions were commensurate, for he stood three feet high at the shoulder, and weighed 150 pounds. His trail, therefore, though obscured by those of his followers, was never difficult to trace. The pack had soon found the track of my drag, and as usual followed it. I could see that Lobo had come to the first bait, sniffed about it, and finally had picked it up.

Then I could not conceal my delight. "I've got him at last," I exclaimed. "I shall find him stark within a mile," and I galloped on with eager eyes fixed on the great broad track in the dust. It led me to the second bait and that also was gone. How I exulted—I surely have him now and perhaps several of his band. But there was the broad pawmark still on the drag, and though I stood in the stirrup and scanned the plain, I saw nothing that looked like a dead wolf. Again I followed—to find now that the third bait was gone—and the king-wolf's track led on to the fourth, there to learn that he had not really taken a bait at all, but had merely carried them in his mouth. Then having piled the three on the fourth, he scattered filth over them to express his utter contempt for my devices. After this, he left my drag and went about his business with the pack he guarded so effectively.

If Lobo's ability to recognize that the meat was poisoned surprised Granddaddy, the wolf's talent for unearthing hidden traps caused nothing short of amazement.

At length the wolf traps arrived, and with two men, I worked a whole week to get them properly set out. We spared no labor or pains. I adopted every device I could think of that might help to insure success. The second day after the traps arrived, I rode around to inspect, and soon came upon Lobo's trail running from trap to trap. In the dust, I could read the whole story of his doings that night. He had trotted along in the darkness, and although the traps were so carefully concealed, he had instantly detected the first one. Stopping the onward march of the pack, he had cautiously scratched around it until he had disclosed the trap, the chain, and the log, then left them wholly exposed to view with the trap still unsprung, and passing on, he treated over a dozen traps in the same fashion. Very soon I noticed that he stopped and turned aside as soon as he detected suspicious signs on the trail, and a new plan to outwit him at once suggested itself. I set the traps in the form of an H; that is, with a row of traps on each side of the trail, and one on the trail for the cross-bar of the H. Before long, I had an opportunity to count another failure. Lobo came trotting along the trail, and was fairly between the parallel lines before he detected the single trap in the trail, but he stopped in time, and why or how he knew enough I cannot tell, the Angel of the wild things must have been with him, but without turning an inch to the right or left, he slowly and cautiously backed on his own tracks, putting each paw exactly in its old track until he was off the dangerous ground. Then returning at one side, he scratched clods and stones with his hind feet till he had sprung every trap.

This he did on many other occasions, and although I varied my methods and redoubled my precautions, he was never deceived, his sagacity seemed never at fault, and he might have been pursuing his career of rapine today, but for an unfortunate alliance that proved his ruin and added his name to the long list of heroes who, unassailable when alone, have fallen through the indiscretion of a trusted ally.

Seton drawing of animal traps

And indeed, Granddaddy did eventually trap Lobo, not because he outsmarted him, but because he tricked Blanca, Lobo's mate. Knowing what a curious she-wolf Blanca was, Granddaddy had placed traps around a cow's head, hoping to draw her in to sniff at the carcass.

Next morning, I sallied forth to inspect the traps, and there, oh, joy! were the tracks of the pack, and the place where the beef-head and its traps had been was empty. A hasty study of the trail showed that Lobo had kept the pack from approaching the meat, but one, a small wolf, had evidently gone on to examine the head as it lay apart and had walked right into one of the traps.

We set out on the trail, and within a mile discovered that the hapless wolf was Blanca. Away she went, however, at a gallop, although encumbered by the beef-head, which weighed over fifty pounds, she speedily distanced my companion who was on foot. But we overtook her when she reached the rocks, for the horns of the cow's head became caught and held her fast. She was the handsomest wolf I had ever seen. Her coat was in perfect condition and nearly white.

She turned to fight, and raising her voice in the rallying cry of her race, sent a long howl rolling over the cañon. From far away upon the mesa came a deep response, the cry of Old Lobo. That was her last call, for now we had closed in on her, and all her energy and breath were devoted to combat.

At intervals during the tragedy, and afterward as we rode homeward, we heard the roar of Lobo as he wandered about on the distant mesas, where he seemed to be searching for Blanca. He had never really deserted her, but knowing that he could not save her, his deep-rooted dread of firearms had been too much for him when he saw us approaching. All that day we heard him wailing as he roamed in his quest, and I remarked at length to one of the boys, "Now, indeed, I truly know that Blanca was his mate."

As evening fell he seemed to be coming toward the home cañon, for his voice sounded continuously nearer. There was an unmistakable note of sorrow in it now. It was no longer the loud, defiant howl, but a long, plaintive wail; "Blanca! Blanca!" he seemed to call. And as night came down, I noticed that he was not far from the place where we had overtaken her. At length he seemed to find the trail, and when he came to the spot where we had killed her, his heart-broken wailing was piteous to hear. It was sadder than I could possibly have believed. Even the stolid cowboys noticed it, and they had "never heard a wolf carry on like that before." He seemed to know exactly what had taken place, for her blood had stained the place of her death.

Lobo never ceased to look for his beloved Blanca and, in doing so, threw all caution to the wind and became entangled in some of Granddaddy's traps. When Granddaddy found Lobo, he carried him back to the ranch and set food and water in front of him. Lobo never moved again.

A lion shorn of his strength, an eagle robbed of his freedom, or a dove bereft of his mate, all die, it is said, of a broken heart; and who will aver that this grim bandit could bear the threefold brunt, heart-whole? This only I know, that when the morning dawned, he was lying there still in his position of calm repose, but his spirit was gone—the old king-wolf was dead.

I took the chain from his neck; a cowboy helped me to carry him to the shed where lay the remains of Blanca, and as we laid him beside her, the cattle-man exclaimed, "There, you would come to her; now you are together again."

Whenever Granddaddy would tell the tale of Lobo, you could tell how affected he was both by Lobo's cunning and by his dedication to Blanca. Granddaddy had hunted the wolf pack that had been killing off the cattle and sheep of the ranchers of Currumpaw, the livestock that provided their livelihood, but while doing so he had discovered an intellect and loyalty in these wild animals that he had perhaps not expected. This was a turning point in Granddaddy's life. In the long time it had taken him to hunt down Lobo, he had formed an attachment to the great wolf. This led to his deep and abiding respect for all living things.

Granddaddy never hunted again.

Seton drawing of Blanca, Lobo, and Lobo's wolf pack

CHAPTER 15

Personal Best

The Chief and Aunt Julie set high standards for the Childervil campers and encouraged each of them to work toward achieving an individual goal. No one competed against another person, just against himself. The projects were challenging.

I was a very talkative child. The Chief and Aunt Julie thought it would help me if I learned to talk less and listen more. I had been given an almost impossible task—not to talk to *anyone* for three days and three nights. This was very hard for me. I would bite my tongue, walk away from people, use sign language, put my hand over my mouth, anything that would help me stay silent. I kept repeating to myself, "Don't talk, don't talk, don't talk—" For two full days I did not utter a sound. On the third day, I forgot.

I had been standing with a group of other children at Childervil. Everyone was talking about the hike we had taken earlier that day. "I can't believe it," one of the campers exclaimed. "I actually saw a rattlesnake! I heard its rattle and looked over to where the sound came from. It was huge! It had just attacked a prairie dog. Otherwise, it might have attacked me!"

"The Chief *killed* a rattlesnake once," I blurted out before remembering I wasn't supposed to be talking. I quickly put my hand over my mouth. Would it matter that I had spoken? It was only a small slip-up. I silently walked away from the group, worried about what would happen.

The next day, when I entered the dining room at lunchtime in eager anticipation of the awards ceremony, I had convinced myself that everything would be fine. The Chief and Aunt Julie knew that I had been trying very hard. They certainly wouldn't hold a few words against me, I thought. After all, I was only seven years old. I couldn't be expected to be perfect.

The Chief walked to the front of the dining room and began the recognition ceremony. "Tommy Oliver, as we all know, is our fastest runner. We challenged him to find ways he could share his strong athletic skills with other campers, coaching them and helping them improve their running form. He did just that. In fact, on a number of occasions, his counselors and I have witnessed him stopping the activity he was involved in to assist fellow campers. Congratulations, Tommy! Let's give him a round of applause. We challenged Mary Muller to find ways to put the needs of others in front of her own. She chose to do this by supervising and caring for our younger campers during classes and on hikes. Great job, Mary! You demonstrated strong leadership skills on top of everything else. Our young campers learned a lot from you, and I know our counselors really appreciated your selfless help. Congratulations on your achievement!" On and on the Chief went, cheering for all the children who had achieved their goals. I listened attentively, waiting to hear my name called. It didn't happen. The Chief was suddenly asking everyone to give a final round of applause to those who had succeeded. He hadn't called my name.

I burst into tears and ran from the dining room. "I'm only seven," I sobbed, "only seven. How can you expect me to be perfect?" I stomped around, kicking dirt everywhere. "I don't want to be here anymore. I want to go home to Los Angeles," I cried and threw myself to the ground. By now I was so upset that my entire body was shaking, and I was gasping for breath.

I looked up and saw Granddaddy standing there. I had not realized he had followed me out of the dining room. I smiled. I was sure he would comfort me by saying he would recognize me anyway. Instead, he sat down on the ground next to me and said, "I'm sorry you're so upset, Chipmunk, but you didn't earn recognition. You didn't finish your project. You can't expect to be rewarded when you haven't earned the reward. Aunt Julie and I can't make an exception for you just because you are only seven or because we love you. I know you had a difficult task, but it's hard work to become a better person. Maybe you'll succeed next time if you remember that it takes great effort to achieve a goal—and that it's something you have to do all by yourself." He kissed me and told me he loved me very much.

Aunt Julie and Granddaddy, New Mexico, 1927

I was young, but I learned an important lesson that day. It would have been easy for Granddaddy or Aunt Julie to have given in to my tears and rewarded me with the recognition I so desired. After all, I had tried; I had succeeded for two full days! Looking back, I am sure it must have been very difficult for them to decide they could not give me an award, since I had not completed my task. When Granddaddy talked to me outside the dining room, it was undoubtedly hard for him to remain firm. That lesson has stayed with me my whole life. I learned it takes great effort to get better at the things that are important—and we aren't always successful the first time we try. I have never forgotten this. Although I was sad and disappointed at the time, it was one of the most valuable lessons I was ever taught.

CHAPTER 16

Plays at Childervil

Script excerpted from *The Wild Animal Play* by Ernest Thompson Seton

During summer camp, the Chief would write plays for the children to perform. Sometimes he used characters from *Wild Animals I Have Known*, *The Trail of the Sandhill Stag*, and *The Biography of a Grizzly.* Then he added things that connected their stories to the College of Indian Wisdom and the Woodcraft League. Many of the animals he made famous were portrayed in these plays: Lobo and Blanca, Bingo, Silverspot, and Redruff. This is part of *The Wild Animal Play.* I got to play Molly Cottontail, Raggylug's mother.

Last of all, cute little Molly Cottontail comes to the front led by Rag. First of all, Rag says:

> I am Raggy, the Cottontail Rabbit,
>   That lived in Old Olifant's Swamp;
> I'm living there yet and, unless it is wet,
>   I'm out every night for a romp.
>
> I was trained in the college of Woodcraft,
>   The college whose hall is in the trees,
> I learned how to swim, play back-tack and limb
>   And puzzle and side-track and freeze.
>
> So well did I study at college,
>   That I know how to baffle my foes;
> For Molly has taught me to run with my wits,
>   And trust in the Sweet Brier-rose.

Seton costume design for Rag

Then Molly says:

> *I am wee, shy Molly Cottontail,*
> *The least of the wildwood band;*
> *I lived with my child in a willow swamp wild,*
> *In the midst of the Sportsman's land.*
>
> *I set all my heart on my baby,*
> *For him I was bold in the strife;*
> *I taught him how wits may be stronger than strength,*
> *And loved him far more than my life.*
>
> *I tricked every big, brutal enemy;*
> *I fought when I ought or I ran,*
> *And at last lost my life when a blizzard was rife,*
> *But I never was ruled by man.*

Molly stamps her foot. Rag and Molly now have their waltz to the music.

Seton costume design for Molly

CHAPTER 17

Memory Hill

"It's going to be the best night ever, isn't it?" I said to Aunt Julie. It was the last full day of summer camp, and there would be an all-night ceremony on the hill behind the Castle, the one that was known as Memory Hill.

Earlier in the day, the Chief had given each of us a rock to paint. "Think about one of your memories of camp," the Chief had directed us, "an Indian design you saw on one of our trips or an animal you remember or something that reminds you of our mountain hike." Children who returned to camp the next year would be allowed to run up Memory Hill to find the rock they created today. It would be a wonderful remembrance of this year's camp experience.

At dusk all of us had carried our rocks up to Memory Hill, solemnly placing them around the area where the council fire would be lit. As we sat down, forming a circle, the Chief told us that this night would be different from other nights at the camp. "Tonight," he said, "I am going to light the council fire without using matches."

A hush came over the group. Most of the campers had *heard* the Chief could do this, but they had never *seen* it happen. *Would the Chief be able to get the fire started?* This was what we were all wondering, although none of us asked the question aloud.

The firewood was laid out, ready to be lit. Next to it was what I called Granddaddy's fire-making tool. Part of it looked like a leather bow, but it didn't have any arrows. The bow was placed around a tall stick that was stuck in a wooden stand. The Chief

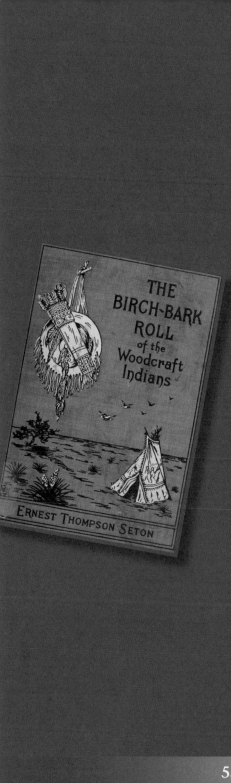

THE BIRCH-BARK ROLL of the Woodcraft Indians

ERNEST THOMPSON SETON

began using the bow to make the stick twirl. Faster and faster went his hands on the bow. Even though I had seen him do this before, I was still anxious. Would the Chief make it work this time? I held my breath in anticipation—and then suddenly there was a spark, a spark that quickly became a flame.

The Chief had started a fire!

I let my breath out. No matter how many times I saw the Chief do this, I was always amazed when the fire actually flamed. Although I didn't say anything to the other campers, I remembered how Granddaddy had once told me stories about fire-making. He said he had made fire this way at least a thousand times. He even thought he held the world's record for doing it quickly—in only thirty-one seconds. The *Guinness Book of Records* didn't exist in the 1930s, but if it had, I'll bet Granddaddy would have been listed in it.

Granddaddy's fire-making tool

The entire night was special. We performed a caribou dance, a Shoshoni dog dance, and an Ojibwa snake dance. We had practiced these for days. I particularly loved the snake dance. In order from tallest to shortest, we held hands and formed a line. Dancing in step to the beat of a drum, we started moving in the line, follow-the-leader style. Eventually, we doubled the line on itself, circling around the fire. Near the end of the dance, we curled tightly around the head of the line. Then the child at the end of the line—who just happened to be me!—jumped on the back of the child in front of him and shook a rattle, like a rattler rattling on its coil.

The Chief had read accounts of the lives of many famous Native American leaders and had been greatly inspired by some of those heroic figures. On Memory Hill he told us stories about Chief Joseph, chief of the Nez Perce; White Calf, chief of the Blackfeet; Dull Knife, a Cheyenne war chief; Tecumseh, war chief of the Shawnees; Kanakuk, a Kickapoo prophet; and Winnemucca, the chief of the Paiutes.

Winnemucca was one of the famous old Chiefs who stood for valor, goodness, and courtesy, and was in himself a noble example of all his own doctrine. . . . He ceaselessly exhorted his people: "To love peace and make constant effort to keep it; always to be kind, one to another; always to tell the truth; and never to take for one's self what belonged to another; to treat old people with tender regard; to care for and help the helpless; to be affectionate in families, and show real respect to women, particularly to mothers."

Throughout the weeks of summer camp, children earned recognition for successes with different projects and activities. On the evening of the final campfire, a special honor was bestowed on one child, who was selected by his group as the most capable and respected camper. He was invited to join the Chief in the inner circle of the council fire.

Seton Dancing Frieze, 1939

After we sang the Arapaho Ghost Dance Song, the Chief explained to the candidate, "Your task is to keep the council fire going until morning. This will mean that you must stay awake all night. If you succeed, you will receive the highest honor of the Woodcraft Indians—the Council Fire Name." It was a very solemn ceremony, and we all took it seriously. At the conclusion, everyone except Johnny Baker, the chosen one, silently walked back to Childervil.

The Chief woke all of us up early the next morning. Together we rushed up the hill to see if the fire was still burning.

"Did you keep your vigil all night long?" the Chief asked.

"I did," replied Johnny.

"Then we can begin the Naming Ceremony."

The Chief had carried two pieces of birch bark with him as he strode up the hill. He held one out for all to see. "Written on this bark are the nicknames your friends and family and teachers have used for you. I now send them into this council fire, and they will vanish with the smoke." We waited while the bark caught fire and became nothing more than ash and smoke.

Seton drawing of pipes

The Chief looked closely at Johnny and held up the second piece of bark. "John Baker, you have excelled in many of our Woodcraft activities: hiking, archery, knot making, and woodcarving. You are learning to read the stars and the phases of the moon, to communicate silently with sign language, and to identify numerous plants and wildlife in this area. You have worked hard to keep yourself physically fit by eating healthy foods and exercising daily. You have proved trustworthy and reliable and courageous. You have shown yourself to be an excellent role model and an outstanding leader. We now award you the highest honor that can be bestowed by this council, the Council Fire Name. On this birch bark, I have written the name we are giving to you. From this day forward, when you are with any member of this group or here at camp, this is the nickname by which you will be known. You have earned this honor, and we congratulate you!"

I knew the Chief was proud of Johnny for successfully completing his challenge. He deserved his Indian nickname.

CHAPTER 18

The Wonders of New Mexico

Sometimes Granddaddy and Aunt Julie would take me on "field trips." During summer camp we took many such excursions, caravanning in several cars to see some of the wonders of New Mexico. On other occasions, it would be just the three of us off on an adventure. Granddaddy loved New Mexico, and he taught me about each of the places we visited. Having spent most of my life in a city, I found all of our trips fascinating.

Carlsbad Caverns

Excerpt of "Atalapha" from *Wild Animal Ways* by Ernest Thompson Seton

"Are we really going to see bats in the caves?" I asked Granddaddy.

"We are indeed," Granddaddy replied.

We were on our way to the famous Carlsbad Caverns. Granddaddy was excited about taking me there. He had told me there were many caves and that they had been part of an ocean reef millions of years ago. There definitely were no oceans in New Mexico when I was there.

I knew the caves were going to be spectacular to see, but I was apprehensive about the bats. "Bats are kind of creepy," I said. "Are there a lot of them in the caves?"

"Yes, Chipmunk," Granddaddy said, "but they're not creepy. Most people who think they are scary associate them with witches and vampires and Halloween. Bats aren't evil; they're really quite interesting."

"What makes them so interesting?" I asked.

"Well," he replied, "for one thing, they are the only mammals that can fly. They help us because they eat lots of insects, including mosquitoes. They are also known for their echolocation."

"Their ec . . . ho . . . what?"

"Their echolocation. It allows them to know where things are even when they can't see them," Granddaddy told me. "Bats use it to find their way in the dark. They also use it to find food. Basically, bats make sounds and then listen for the echoes of these sounds as they bounce off objects. This helps them figure out how big the object is, how far away it is, and whether it is moving or not."

Seton pen and ink drawing of bat

"I wish I had echo . . . lo . . ."

"Echolocation. Yes, it would be useful, wouldn't it? For me, too—I could go to the library to write in the middle of the night without bumping into objects or waking anyone up by turning on all the lights."

"I don't think I'd be afraid of the dark if I had echo . . . location," I replied thoughtfully. I looked up at Granddaddy. "Can you tell me about *baby* bats?" I asked.

"Well, the babies are called pups. Sometimes they grow up in nursery colonies. There can be hundreds of pups in one little area of a cave ceiling—an area smaller than one of those big books in my library. Being that close together keeps them all warm, and then they grow faster. They are usually fully grown by the time they are only six to nine weeks old. Mother bats are very smart. Even though four or five hundred pups may be together in such tight quarters, the momma bat can find her own pup when she returns to the cave with food. No one is quite sure how this is possible, but it's true."

"Could you find me if I was with five hundred other little girls, Granddaddy?"

"Of course I could, Chipmunk," he answered. "I love you. I would always be able to find you." We drove in silence for a little while. Then I asked Granddaddy if he knew any bat stories.

"I do," he said. "A few years ago, I wrote a book with a story about bats in it. I think they are a lot like the magical brownies in fairy tales. Brownies are two-legged elfins with fur cloaks and sharp-pointed ears. They prance over the treetops on moonlit nights, and they are very friendly to man. They usually live in caves and hide all day. They often sleep or hibernate during the winter. And of course, they can fly in the dark."

"That's echolocation!" I cried.

"Smart girl!" he said. "Well, the bat I wrote about in *Wild Animal Ways* was called Atalapha, and he was a winged brownie. When he was young, he was called Brother or Big Brother, and his twin was called Little Brother. I think I'll tell you about their first flying lessons and how they learned to catch food in mid-air."

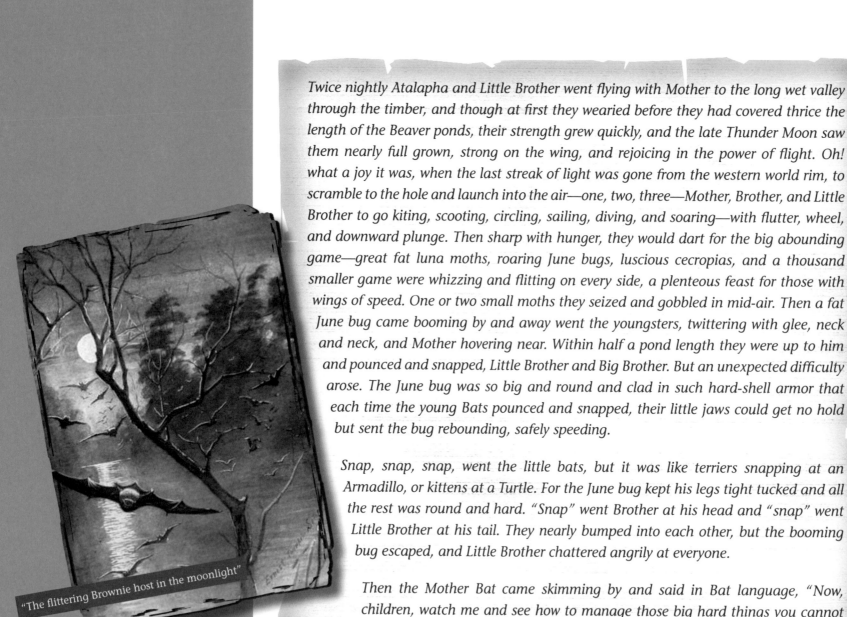

"The flittering Brownie host in the moonlight"

Twice nightly Atalapha and Little Brother went flying with Mother to the long wet valley through the timber, and though at first they wearied before they had covered thrice the length of the Beaver ponds, their strength grew quickly, and the late Thunder Moon saw them nearly full grown, strong on the wing, and rejoicing in the power of flight. Oh! what a joy it was, when the last streak of light was gone from the western world rim, to scramble to the hole and launch into the air—one, two, three—Mother, Brother, and Little Brother to go kiting, scooting, circling, sailing, diving, and soaring—with flutter, wheel, and downward plunge. Then sharp with hunger, they would dart for the big abounding game—great fat luna moths, roaring June bugs, luscious cecropias, and a thousand smaller game were whizzing and flitting on every side, a plenteous feast for those with wings of speed. One or two small moths they seized and gobbled in mid-air. Then a fat June bug came booming by and away went the youngsters, twittering with glee, neck and neck, and Mother hovering near. Within half a pond length they were up to him and pounced and snapped, Little Brother and Big Brother. But an unexpected difficulty arose. The June bug was so big and round and clad in such hard-shell armor that each time the young Bats pounced and snapped, their little jaws could get no hold but sent the bug rebounding, safely speeding.

Snap, snap, snap, went the little bats, but it was like terriers snapping at an Armadillo, or kittens at a Turtle. For the June bug kept his legs tight tucked and all the rest was round and hard. "Snap" went Brother at his head and "snap" went Little Brother at his tail. They nearly bumped into each other, but the booming bug escaped, and Little Brother chattered angrily at everyone.

Then the Mother Bat came skimming by and said in Bat language, "Now, children, watch me and see how to manage those big hard things you cannot bite." She swooped after the roaring bug, but making no attempt to use her teeth, she sailed over, then in a twinkling curled her tail with its broad flap into a bag, and scooped the June bug in. Her legs helped to close the net; a quick reach back of the supple neck *and the boomer was seized by the head. Her hind feet clutched it firmly; a few quick movements of her jaws, the wing cases, the armored legs and horns went down rattling into the leafage, and the June bug's body was like a chicken trussed for eating, cleaned of all but the meat.*

Calling to the twins with a twittering squeak, she took a fat lump in her teeth and flew onward and upward, still calling. Then as they labored in pursuit, she rose a little and dropped the big luscious prize.

Away went Brother, and after went Little Brother, in pursuit of falling food. It fell straight; they darted in zigzags. Again and again they struck at it, but could not hold it. It was surely falling to the ground, where it would be lost, for no Frosted Bat would eat food from the ground. But Mother swooped, and with her tail scooped the round thing in again.

Once more she flew to the higher level above the trees. Again she called to the brothers to try their powers. And as the fat body dropped a second time, they resumed their eager zigzags. A little screech of joy from Little Brother announced that he had scooped the body, but he lost his wing balance and dropped the June bug to recover himself. It had not fallen twenty feet before Brother dashed under, sideways and up, then twittered in needle tones of joy, for he had won the prize and won it in fair play. The old Bat would have eaten it on the wing, but the little ones were not yet steady enough for that, so they flew to a tall tree, and to a top branch, which afforded a good perch, and they reveled in the spoils.

"Tell me more," I cried.

"On the way home," Granddaddy replied. "Now we've arrived at the caves, so we're actually going to see the bats."

Visiting the Carlsbad Caverns was, as Granddaddy had predicted, amazing. I did see bats, but I also saw all the speleothem growing in the caves. Speleothem are the minerals that form when water drips or seeps in or flows in the caves. Stalactites hang from the ceilings of the caves. Stalagmites grow up from the ground. There are also crystals. Speleothem have funny names like broomstick, popcorn, cave pearls, fried eggs, soda straws, and totem poles. This was one of the best trips that I took with Granddaddy and Aunt Julie. Many years later I related my memories of the visit to my own children, showing them pictures of the caves in books we checked out of the public library.

Acoma Pueblo

Acoma Creation Story retold from a myth written down by Matthew W. Stirling in 1928. He obtained it from a group of Acomas visiting Washington, D.C.

We visited Taos and Acoma Pueblos, villages where hundreds of years earlier the Pueblo Indians had constructed buildings out of water, dirt, and straw. They reminded me of Seton Village. We also saw cliff dwellings where Native Americans had carved out places to live in the high walls of the canyons. They were astonishing and unlike any houses I had ever seen. Granddaddy explained that these took many

Acoma Pueblo

years to build and were always expanding as the number of people living in them grew. Indians built their homes in such locations because it made it harder for their enemies to reach them.

Of all the pueblos, Acoma was my favorite. Built at the top of a great sandstone mesa, it is now known as "Sky City." The Pueblo people have lived at Acoma Pueblo for almost nine hundred years, making it the oldest continuously inhabited community in the United States. (Another *oldest!*) For a very long time, the people who lived in the pueblo had to climb up a deep canyon trail with only handholds to keep them on the narrow path as they transported their water and other needed supplies. There is now a road up to the city, but there is still no electricity or running water, and the only bathrooms are outhouses. Food is still cooked in outdoor beehive ovens.

Behive oven at Acoma Pueblo

On the way home from one of our visits to Acoma, Granddaddy said to me, "You know, Chipmunk, all cultures have creation stories—stories about how their world was created and how its people came to be. Today, while your aunt drives us back to Seton Village, I will tell you the story the Acoma people tell about their beginnings."

Two sisters, Nautsiti and Iatiku, were born in a dark world beneath the earth called Shipapu. For many, many moons, they lived in this world, speaking only to the Spirit Tsichtinako. One day they found a gift from Tsichtinako: two baskets of seeds and the pictures of the animals that would be above ground. They planted the four types of seeds and these sprouted into strong pine trees. After many, many years, one of the trees poked a hole through the earth. Unfortunately, the hole was not big enough for the sisters to squeeze through. Tsichtinako told the sisters to look in their baskets, find the picture of the badger, and tell it to become alive. It crawled up the tree and gnawed a hole big enough for the sisters to pass through.

"Take your baskets with you," Tsichtinako directed the sisters, "and crawl out through the hole. Your father left you everything in the baskets so that you can help him complete the world."

After thanking the Sun for the light, Nautsiti and Iatiku planted seeds for corn. When the corn ripened, their father sent them fire so they could cook the corn. Soon they planted many other seeds and gave life to a variety of animals—first to small animals like the kangaroo mouse, the mole, and the prairie dog. Later they gave life to cottontail rabbits, antelope, and deer, then to elk, bison, and bears. They let loose birds to fly in the air and fish to swim in the rivers. They planted grasses and made mountains. They planted seeds for piñon, cedar, oak, and walnut trees.

Tsichtinako had warned Nautsiti and Iatiku to be careful with their baskets. For a while they were very cautious. In time, however, they got so excited about giving life to plants and creatures that they became careless. One day they dropped the image of an animal from one of the baskets, and the image came alive on its own—a strange and powerful snake. The minute the serpent had life in its body, it tempted the sisters, and they began to argue. They started making plans for how they could out-do each other. Neither sister was happy any longer. After a while, they decided they should no longer live with each other. They would divide what was in their baskets and go their separate ways. But even then, they could not agree. Iatiku did not want the seeds for the fruits and vegetables or the animals that Nautsiti offered; she said that sheep and cattle and wheat were too much work to raise. Finally, deeply saddened that her sister did not want her offerings, Nautsiti left for the East.

Iatiku stayed in the West. She had many children, and they called themselves the Sun Clan, the first of the clans to live at Acoma.

Cerrillos Mines, the Petroglyphs, and Other Trips

I enjoyed many other trips, including one to the Cerrillos Mines and one to see the petroglyphs near Albuquerque. Petroglyphs are rock carvings made by pecking away at the hard rock surface. Often a stone chisel was used and was hit with another stone that acted as a hammer. Many of the thousands of petroglyphs were created four hundred to seven hundred years ago.

They were carved by Pueblo Indians and, even though they look like pictures, many can only be understood by the Puebloan people. These picture carvings captivated me. Granddaddy gave me some paper and a pencil, and I tried to copy some of them. When we returned to Seton Village, I spent days re-creating some of the petroglyphs on paper. I even sharpened a small rock and tried to carve some petroglyphs on large rocks. It was very hard work, but I did manage to carve the outline of a horse and another of a bird.

Some of the best trips were the ones when we traveled to Native American villages in New Mexico and the surrounding states. Granddaddy was good friends with many Indian leaders, and we were always treated like special visitors. I learned a lot about the cultures of the various Native American tribes in the Southwest and the Great Plains. I loved to watch the Indians dancing in their beautiful colorful costumes, and I learned how to do the corn dance and the rain dance. I also learned how to bake bread and make baskets, pottery, and clothing. I told Granddaddy and Aunt Julie that when I grew up, I wanted to be an Indian!

By the time I lived in Santa Fe, most of the turquoise mines had been closed, but Granddaddy took me to visit the Cerrillos mines anyway, since they were only a dozen or so miles from Seton Village. He told me how the Puebloans had worked the mines for hundreds of years. Later, Spanish settlers and others, including Tiffany, the big

Petroglyph National Monument

New York jewelry store, had mined a major part of the Cerrillos mines. Tiffany alone extracted over two million dollars worth of turquoise from the mines in the late 1800s. That was a lot of money back then.

Granddaddy always remembered how much I loved the trip to Cerrillos. Because of this, when I left Santa Fe to return permanently to California, he and Aunt Julie bought me a very special gift: a beautiful turquoise and silver necklace. Although Granddaddy and Aunt Julie published a lot of books and lectured around the country, they never had a lot of money. Much of what they made went to support the College of Indian Wisdom—they were always constructing new buildings and hiring well-known teachers. The necklace was such a generous and unexpected present, and I have always cherished it. It reminds me of how much Granddaddy and Aunt Julie loved me. It also brings back memories of our visit to the Cerrillos turquoise mines and many of the other wonderful places we traveled to.

Cerrillos Hills and some of the turquoise found in the hills

CHAPTER 19

Quicksight and the Moccasin Game

"**M**y board is ready, Chipmunk. Look quickly!" Granddaddy had arranged five nuts and five pebbles on his Quicksight board. "One . . . two . . . three . . . four . . . five . . ." he counted before laying a piece of paper over his board. It was my turn to duplicate his design—from memory!

When I first lived at Seton Village, this was a very difficult game for me to play. Granddaddy had taught it to me by using a smaller board with only twelve squares and four counters, but my powers of observation developed quickly and soon I was able to play with the full board and all ten counters, almost always getting the pattern right.

Aunt Julie would play a variation of Quicksight with me, one in which she would grab a basketful of silverware and other utensils from the kitchen. Sometimes she would put out a dozen or so items and then have me close my eyes while she removed one. I would have to figure out which object she had taken away. At first, she would leave all the items in the same place and just take one away, but as I got better at the game, she would mix up the remaining objects; then it became more difficult to figure out which item was no longer there. Some days Aunt Julie would just put ten or so rocks, flowers, feathers, and similar objects on the table, give me five seconds to look at them, scoop them all into her basket, and ask me what the ten objects had been. This meant I had to know the names of different rocks and the difference between the feather of a pinyon jay and that of a great blue heron.

Quicksight Game

counters

I loved Quicksight but my absolute favorite game was the Moccasin Game that Granddaddy and I played often. It was another game that required me to pay very close attention. H. Clark Brown, a well-known naturalist and writer who spent several summers at the College of Indian Wisdom, wrote a poem about our game in his book *Child Life in Seton Village.*

Seton teepee drawings

THE MOCCASIN GAME
  by H. Clark Brown

Now Leila calls to Chief to come
    and play a game with her.
"I've got the moccasins," she says,
    "and there's an awful stir
Among the horses. Come, you see,
    we'll stand them in a row
On either side, and I will let
    you start the game." And so,

The Chieftain takes the hiding stone
    and down upon their knees,
The two of them begin, and if
    the cublet ever sees
The stone within the hider's hand,
    she gives no sign at all,
Until his song is ended and
    he puts his hairy paws
In front of her to guess the one
    or find the moccasin
Where he might put it. And she pats
    the hand that it is in.

And thus her turn has come, and so,
  because she won, she takes,
One of the long white sticks which is
  the horse the Chief forsakes.
Then she will hide it while she sings,
  and Chief will watch so close
Her little flitting hands that he
  will see the stone—almost.
But now the song is done, and he
  will sniff and sniff to see
If hand or moccasin betrays
  the place where the stone may be.

And so they play the moccasin game
  a summer's afternoon,
And as they play, they sing away
  on many an eyrie tune.
And horses change from the Chieftain's side
  to Leila's, until all
Become her property, and then—
  there often comes a call
To run to other things to do
  and horses stay in play
Within the corral Leila owns,
  until another day.

Seton teepee drawings

I am still very good at observing something quickly and remembering exactly what I saw. I think it's due to my early training with Granddaddy and Aunt Julie.

CHAPTER 20

On the Road: Beyond New Mexico

Sometimes our travels took us further afield. Each fall Granddaddy and Aunt Julie would travel around the United States—and even to Canada. They would lecture about Native American customs and culture, talk about the College of Indian Wisdom, and discuss the Woodcraft League of America. Into all of this, Granddaddy, always the storyteller, would weave his stories.

Seton untitled row of teepees

Cheyenne   Gray-Wolf (Crow)   Blackfoot   Omaha

The first time Aunt Julie and Granddaddy spoke about a planned tour, I was worried. I was afraid I would be left at home in Seton Village. I liked our housekeeper, Maria, but I wanted to be with Granddaddy and Aunt Julie. They told me I could go with them, but they warned me that I must be well behaved and explained that sometimes

I would have to stay in a hotel room all by myself. I had only stayed in a hotel once before, with Aunt Julie on the way from Needles to Santa Fe. It was still such a new and exciting experience, I told them I wouldn't mind. We went to other cities in New Mexico and to cities in Texas and California. I had never left Los Angeles before I moved to New Mexico; suddenly, I was visiting places I had not even known existed.

If Aunt Julie and Granddaddy were lecturing at a school or college or other public place, they would take me with them. I liked seeing the people and listening to Granddaddy tell his stories. There would be food served at some of the events, and I particularly enjoyed the little cakes called *petit fours*. When the lecture was in a private home and I couldn't accompany them, I would stay at the hotel under the watchful eye of the desk clerk and wait with anticipation for Granddaddy and Aunt Julie to return. Then Granddaddy would take me onto his lap and tell me an exciting story, always one I had never before heard. The best part was that he would do voices for all the animals, sometimes howling like a coyote or growling like a bear. On the day he told the story of *The Slum Cat*, he yowled liked each of the different cats.

CHAPTER 21

"The Slum Cat"

Story excerpted from *Animal Hereos* by Ernest Thompson Seton

Sometimes the stories Granddaddy would tell were about cats or dogs. One of these cats was a feral kitty called Slum Kitty, later known as Slum Cat. This is the story of how Slum Kitty became friends with Yellow Tom after Yellow's fight with the Black One.

Kitty was now full grown. She was a striking-looking Cat of the tiger type. Her marks were black on a very pale gray, and the four beauty-spots of white on her nose, ears, and tail-tip lent a certain distinction. She was very expert at getting a living, and yet she had some days of starvation and failed in her ambition of catching a sparrow. She was quite alone, but a new force was coming into her life.

She was lying in the sun one August day when a large Black Cat came walking along the top of a wall in her direction. She recognized him at once by his torn ear. She slunk into her box and hid. He picked his way gingerly, bounded lightly to a shed that was at the end of the yard, and was crossing the roof when a Yellow Cat rose up. The Black Tom glared and growled; so did the Yellow Tom. Their tails lashed from side to side. Strong throats growled and yowled. They approached each other with ears laid back, with muscles a-tense.

At this point Granddaddy tensed his muscles, threw back his head and let out the sounds of angry feral cats.

"Yow—yow—ow!" said the Black One.

"Wow—w—w!" was the slightly deeper answer.

"Ya—wow—wow—wow!" said the Black One, edging up half an inch nearer.

"Yow—w—w!" was the Yellow answer, as the blond Cat rose to full height and stepped with vast dignity a whole inch forward. "Yow—w!" and he went another inch, while his tail went swish, thump, from one side to the other.

"Ya—wow—yow—w!" screamed the Black in a rising tone, and he backed the eighth of an inch as he marked the broad, unshrinking breast before him.

Windows opened all around; human voices were heard, but the Cat scene went on.

"Yow-yow-ow!" rumbled the Yellow Peril, his voice deepening as the other's rose. "Yow!" and he advanced another step.

Now their noses were but three inches apart; they stood sidewise, both ready to clinch, but each waiting for the other. They glared for three minutes in silence and like statues, except that each tail-tip was twisting.

The Yellow began again, "Yow—ow—ow!" in deep tone.

"Ya—a—a—a!" screamed the Black, with intent to strike terror by his yell, but he retreated one-sixteenth of an inch. The Yellow walked up a long half-inch; their whiskers were mixing now; another advance and their noses touched.

Granddaddy set me down on the floor in front of him. He pulled himself up to his full six-foot height, bent his fingers to imitate claws and, in his deepest voice, roared, "Yo—w—w!" I sat entranced, waiting anxiously to find out what happened to the cats, especially Slum Kitty, hidden behind her box.

"'Yo-ow!' rumbled the Yellow One."

"Yo—w—w!" said Yellow, like a deep moan.

"Y—a—a—a—a—a!" screamed the Black, but he retreated a thirty-second of an inch, and the Yellow Warrior closed and clinched like a demon.

Oh, how they rolled and bit and tore, especially the Yellow One!

Over and over, sometimes one on top, sometimes another, but mostly the Yellow One, and farther till they rolled off the roof, amid cheers from all the windows. They lost not a second in the fall to the junk-yard; they tore and clawed all the way down, but especially the Yellow One. And when they struck the ground, still fighting, the one on top was chiefly the Yellow One; and before they separated, both had had as much as they wanted, especially the Black One! He scaled a wall and, bleeding and growling, disappeared, while the news was passed from window to window that Cayley's Black had been licked at last by Orange Billy.

Either the Yellow Cat was a very clever seeker, or else Slum Kitty did not hide very hard, but he discovered her among the boxes, and she made no attempt to get away, probably because she had witnessed the fight. There is nothing like success in warfare to win the female heart, and thereafter the Yellow Tom and Kitty became very good friends, not sharing each other's lives or food— Cats do not do that way much—but recognizing each other as entitled to special friendly privileges.

CHAPTER 22

Hogan and Kiva

If anything rivaled Granddaddy's love of nature, it was his immense respect for the First Peoples of the Americas. He and Aunt Julie were working on the first edition of *The Gospel of the Redman*, a book about the wisdom, customs, and traditions of Native Americans, while I was living in Santa Fe. Seton Castle was filled not just with artwork depicting the natural world, but also with the drawings and paintings Granddaddy had produced of Native American canoes, painted paddles, drums and rattles, teepees, moccasins, shields, and headdresses. The bright colors appealed to me as a child, and I spent hours asking Granddaddy to tell me about them and about some of the Indian heroes he wrote about: Hiawatha, Sitting Bull, Crazy Horse, Geronimo, and Powhatan. Several of Granddaddy's books were written because of his high regard for Native American traditions: *The Book of Woodcraft*, *Rolf in the Woods*, and *Two Little Savages*.

His admiration for the First Peoples led Granddaddy to build both a Navajo hogan and a Pueblo kiva during the years I lived in Seton Village. He visited many pueblos and Navajo villages and studied the architecture of the buildings. His journals are full of the measurements and drawings he made during those trips. He felt very honored to be one of the few "white men" allowed inside a sacred Pueblo kiva.

Seton paddle and canoe drawings

A hogan is a traditional Navajo dwelling that is often circular. Sometimes it is shaped like a cone or is a six- or eight-sided building with a domed roof. It usually has a wood frame and is covered with tree bark or grass and mud. The doorway faces east so that the morning sun can warm the house. Navajo people still have hogans that they use for special ceremonies, like the Blessingway. The Blessingway chant is used to bring good luck, good health, and blessings. During the Blessingway ritual, the Navajo sing of the creation of their four original clans.

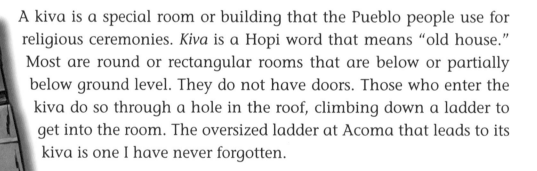

A Navajo Hogan

Granddaddy built the hogan at Seton Village to be used for council fires, dance demonstrations, and Woodcraft ceremonies. He got a very famous Kiowa painter, Jack Hokeah, to paint murals on the inside—lively and colorful paintings of kachinas, Kiowa dancers and singers, and buffalo hunters of the Great Plains. They were beautiful!

A kiva is a special room or building that the Pueblo people use for religious ceremonies. *Kiva* is a Hopi word that means "old house." Most are round or rectangular rooms that are below or partially below ground level. They do not have doors. Those who enter the kiva do so through a hole in the roof, climbing down a ladder to get into the room. The oversized ladder at Acoma that leads to its kiva is one I have never forgotten.

Kiva at Acoma Pueblo

During a visit to the San Ildefonso Pueblo, Granddaddy made drawings and took measurements of its kiva. He copied these into his journal and used them when he designed the Seton Village kiva.

Like the San Ildefonso kiva, the one Granddaddy built was round and included a stairway leading to the roof. From the roof, one climbed down a ladder into the gathering space.

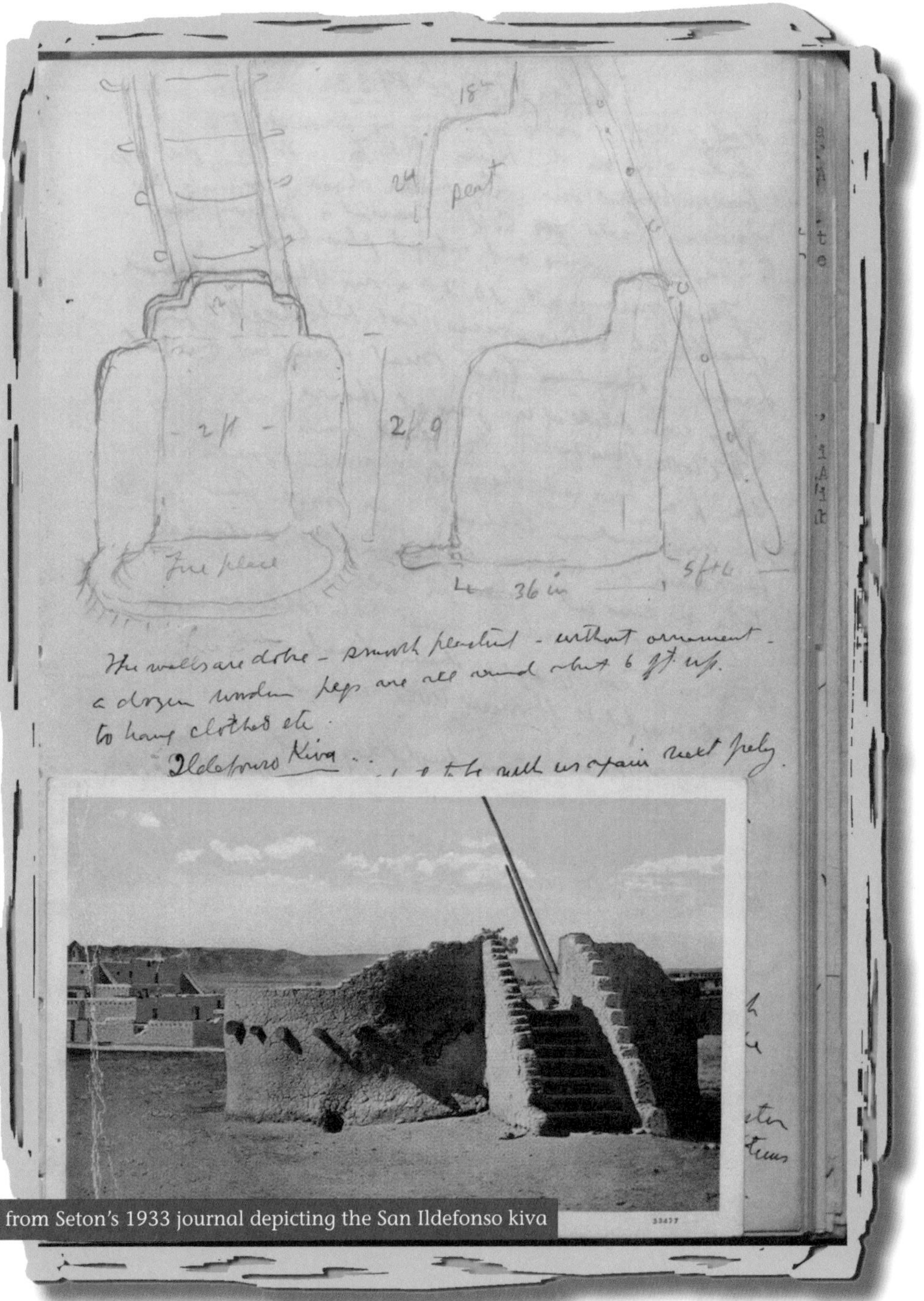

18"

peat

24

2/1

2/9

Fire place

36 in

5ft 6

The walls are adobe — smooth plastered — without ornament.
a dozen wooden pegs are all round about 6 ft up.
to hang clothes etc.

"Ildefonso Kiva ... ... to be with us again next July.

Page from Seton's 1933 journal depicting the San Ildefonso kiva

Juan Gonzales, a medicine man from San Ildefonso, was the construction manager for the project. I attended the ceremony on July 2, 1933, the opening day of camp that year, when Juan blessed the kiva and named it *Pai-o-té-e,* meaning "Summer Kiva." At the celebration that followed the dedication, Jack Hokeah and some of his friends performed Kiowa dances.

On a recent visit to Seton Village, I hiked through desert brush to look at the ruins of the hogan and the kiva. Both buildings have been neglected for many years. The murals inside are faded, and the exterior walls are weather-beaten and pitted with the signs of passing time. Gazing at them, I caught a glimpse of long ago, when workers were constructing these buildings. There I was, a small child standing hand in hand with Granddaddy as he carefully explained to his little Chipmunk the ins and outs of the designs.

Ruins of the Seton Villiage hogan (top) and kiva (bottom). Although it is faded, you can still see Jack Hokeah's fresco depicting the Eagle Dance.

CHAPTER 23

"Johnny Bear"

Story excerpted with slight adaptations from
Lives of the Hunted by Ernest Thompson Seton

Granddaddy often entertained me with tales about Johnny Bear, a rather spoiled and unruly Black Bear cub that lived in Yellowstone Park. Granddaddy had spent time in Yellowstone, watching and photographing the group of bears who cadged food from the garbage dump near the famous Fountain Hotel. (Of course, nowadays, we know that it is unhealthy for bears to eat people food, but no one really understood this more than a hundred years ago.) One of the best Johnny Bear stories Granddaddy told was the one about the day Johnny—and Granddaddy—encountered a monster grizzly bear.

Johnny was a queer little bear cub that lived with Grumpy, his mother, in Yellowstone Park. Grumpy was the biggest and fiercest of the Black Bears, and Johnny, apparently her only son, was a peculiarly tiresome little cub, for he seemed never to cease either grumbling or whining. They were among the many Bears that found a desirable home in the country about the Fountain Hotel. The steward of the hotel had ordered the kitchen garbage to be dumped in an open glade of the surrounding forest, thus providing, throughout the season, a daily feast for the Bears.

It was in the summer of 1897 that I made their acquaintance. I was in the park to study the home life of the animals and had been told that in the woods near the Fountain Hotel, I could see Bears at any time if I should go to the garbage heap, a quarter-mile off in the forest.

Early the next morning, I went to this Bears' Banqueting Hall in the pines and hid in the near bushes. All morning the Bears came and went or wandered near my hiding-place without discovering me, and except for one or two brief quarrels, there was nothing very exciting to note. But about three in the afternoon, it became more lively.

My eye caught a movement on the hilltop whence all the Bears had come, and out stalked a very large Black Bear with a tiny cub. It was Grumpy and Little Johnny. The old Bear stalked down the slope toward the feast, and Johnny hitched alongside, grumbling as he came, his mother watching him as solicitously as ever a hen did her single chick. Johnny had evidently been there before now, for he seemed to know quite well the staple kinds of canned goods. A large syrup-can made him happy for a long time. It had had a lid, so that the hole was round and smooth, but it was not big enough to admit his head, and he could not touch its riches with his tongue stretched out its longest. He soon hit on a plan, however. Putting in his little black arm, he churned it around, then drew out and licked it clean; and while he licked one he got the other one ready; and he did this again and again, until the can was as clean inside as when first it had left the factory.

All the jam-pots were at Johnny's end; he stayed by them, and Grumpy stayed by him. At length he noticed that his mother had a better tin than any he could find, and as he ran whining to take it from her, he chanced to glance away up the slope. There he saw something that made him sit up and utter a curious Koff Koff Koff Koff.

His mother turned quickly and sat up to see "what the child was looking at." I followed their gaze and there, oh, horrors! was an enormous Grizzly Bear. He was a monster; he looked like a fur-clad omnibus coming through the trees. Johnny set up a whine at once and got behind his mother. She uttered a deep growl and all her black hair stood on end. Mine did too, but I kept as still as possible. With stately tread, the Grizzly came on. His vast shoulders sliding along his sides, and his silvery robe swaying at each tread, like the trappings on an elephant, gave an impression of power that was appalling.

"A syrup-tin kept him happy for a long time."

Johnny began to whine more loudly, and I fully sympathized with him now, though I did not join in. After a moment's hesitation, Grumpy turned to her noisy cub and said something that sounded to me like two or three short coughs—Koff, Koff, Koff. But I imagine that she really said, "My child, I think you had better get up that tree, while I go and drive the brute away."

At any rate, that was what Johnny did, and this what she set out to do. But Johnny had no notion of missing any fun. He wanted to see what was going to happen. So he did not rest contented where he was hidden in the thick branches of the pine, but combined safety with view by climbing to the topmost branch that would bear him, and there, sharp against the sky, he squirmed about and squealed aloud in his excitement. The branch was so small that it bent under his weight, swaying this way and that as he shifted about, and every moment I expected to see it snap off. If it had been broken when swaying my way, Johnny would certainly have fallen on me, and this would probably have resulted in bad feelings between myself and his mother; but the limb was tougher than it looked, or perhaps Johnny had had plenty of experience, for he neither lost his hold nor broke his branch.

Meanwhile, Grumpy stalked out to meet the Grizzly. She stood as high as she could and set her bristles on end; then, growling and chopping her teeth, she faced him.

The Grizzly, so far as I could see, took no notice of her. He came striding toward the feast as though alone. But when Grumpy got within twelve feet of him, she uttered a succession of short, coughy roars, and, charging, gave him a tremendous blow on the ear. The Grizzly was surprised, but he replied with a left-hander that knocked her over like a sack of hay.

Nothing daunted, but doubly furious, she jumped up and rushed at him. Then they clinched and rolled over and over, whacking and pounding, snorting and growling, and making no end of dust and rumpus. But above all their noise, I could clearly hear Little Johnny, yelling at the top of his voice and evidently encouraging his mother to go right in and finish the Grizzly at once.

Why the Grizzly did not break her in two, I could not understand. After a few minutes' struggle, during which I could see nothing but dust and dim flying legs, the two separated as by mutual consent—perhaps the regulation time was up—and for a while they stood glaring at each other, Grumpy at least much winded.

The Grizzly would have dropped the matter right there. He did not wish to fight. He had no idea of troubling himself about Johnny. All he wanted was a quiet meal. But no! The moment he took one step toward the garbage-pile—that is, as Grumpy thought, toward Johnny—she went at him again. But this time the Grizzly was ready for her. With one blow, he knocked her off her feet and sent her crashing on to a huge upturned pine-root. She was fairly staggered this time. The force of the blow, and the rude reception of the rooty antlers, seemed to take all the fight out of her. She scrambled over and tried to escape. But the Grizzly was mad now. He meant to punish her and dashed around the root. For a minute they kept up a dodging chase about it, but Grumpy was quicker of foot and somehow always managed to keep the root between herself and her foe, while Johnny, safe in the tree, continued to take an intense and uproarious interest.

At length, seeing he could not catch her that way, the Grizzly sat up on his haunches; and while he doubtless was planning a new move, old Grumpy saw her chance, and making a dash got away from the root and up to the top of the tree where Johnny was perched.

Having photographed this interesting group from my hiding-place, I thought I must get a closer picture at any price, and for the first time in the day's proceedings, I jumped out of the hole and ran under the tree. I was close to the trunk and was peering about and seeking for a chance to use the camera when old Grumpy began to come down, chopping her teeth and uttering her threatening cough at me. She slowly came down from branch to branch, growling and threatening. But when she neared the ground, she kept on the far side of the trunk and finally slipped down and ran into the woods without the slightest pretense of carrying out any of her dreadful threats. Thus Johnny was again left alone. He climbed up to his old perch and resumed his monotonous whining.

What became of Grumpy the rest of that day, I do not know. Johnny, after bewailing for a time, realized that there was no sympathetic hearer of his cries, and therefore very sagaciously stopped them. Having no mother now to plan for him, he began to plan for himself and at once proved that he was better stuff than he seemed. After watching, with a look of profound cunning on his little black face, and waiting till the Grizzly was some distance away, he silently slipped down behind the trunk, and ran like a hare to the next tree, never stopping to breathe till he was on its topmost bough. For he was thoroughly convinced that the only object that the Grizzly had in life was to kill him, and he seemed quite aware that his enemy could not climb a tree.

"Johnny got behind his mother."

Another long and safe survey of the Grizzly, who really paid no heed to him whatever, was followed by another dash for the next tree, varied occasionally by a cunning feint to mislead the foe. So he went dashing from tree to tree and climbing each to its very top, although it might be but ten feet from the last, till he disappeared in the woods. After perhaps ten minutes, his voice again came floating on the breeze, the habitual querulous whining, which told me he had found his mother and had resumed his customary appeal to her sympathy.

CHAPTER 24

Visitors to the Castle

Many famous people came to visit Granddaddy. He and Aunt Julie entertained Indian chiefs, artists, writers, singers, dancers, and professors. Sometimes when Indian chiefs came, Granddaddy smoked peace pipes with them. Many times he spoke to them in sign language. A few of the visitors who came to the Castle included:

Renowned Native American potter **Maria Martinez** of the San Ildefonso Pueblo re-created the black-on-black pottery that the ancient Pueblo had once crafted. She worked side by side with her husband, Julian, who developed the paint used on the blackware and fashioned the beautiful designs painted on the pots. My aunt and uncle had a collection of Maria Martinez pottery.

Like Granddaddy, **Mary Austin** was a nature writer. She was deeply interested in Native American cultures also and spent many years studying the traditions of the Indians of the Mojave Desert. Because she was such good friends with Granddaddy, she served as one of his two references when he applied for and was granted US citizenship in the early 1930s.

Jack Hokeah was one of the famous Native American artists who frequently visited Seton Village. Part of a group of painters called the Kiowa Five, his work was displayed internationally. He loved to sing and dance, and I remember him doing both during his visits. He painted murals in Santa Fe at the US Indian School. He also painted the interior of the hogan at Seton Village while I was living at the Castle.

Chickasaw princess **Te Ata** was often a guest at Seton Village and a lecturer at the College of Indian Wisdom. Like Granddaddy, she was a renowned storyteller and would mesmerize her audience as she told her stories using music and dance. Te Ata's husband, George Clyde Fisher, Director of the Hayden Planetarium at the American Museum of Natural History and a good friend of Granddaddy's, sometimes accompanied her. An avid photographer, he once filmed a Seton Institute trip, capturing footage of Indian dancing at several pueblos.

Gerald Cassidy was an artist and a founding member of the famous Santa Fe Artists Colony. Many of his paintings, including *The Eagle Dancer* and *Buffalo Dancer,* were of Native Americans. These paintings and eight others still grace the walls of La Fonda. Gerald's wife, Ina Sizer Cassidy, was a well-known writer of short stories, poetry, and articles on art. For many years, she wrote a monthly column for *New Mexico Magazine.* She and her husband were very good friends with Granddaddy and Aunt Julie.

Clement Marot Hull was a famous potter who, as a young man, was often at Seton Castle. His family moved to Santa Fe during the years I lived there, when Clem was in his teens. The Hulls became good friends with Granddaddy. After Clem graduated from high school, he and his father set up the Hull-Santa Fe Pottery. There, and later at the Van Briggle Pottery in Colorado, he created some of the finest American ceramics of the twentieth century.

CHAPTER 25
To Stay or Not to Stay

During the third year I lived with Aunt Julie and Granddaddy, my parents came to visit me in New Mexico. They explained to me that my aunt and Seton wanted to adopt me and have me live with them permanently. They told me how very much they loved me but that they knew Aunt Julie and Granddaddy loved me too. Even though I wasn't quite nine years old, they left the decision up to me.

I loved them all: my mother, my father, my aunt, and Granddaddy. And I loved New Mexico. I missed my parents, but I would miss Aunt Julie and Granddaddy if I left. How could I possibly choose? I went to my room and sat on my bed, not sure what I should do.

I thought about all the things I loved about being in New Mexico with Granddaddy and Aunt Julie: the beautiful country, the trips to pueblos, the smell of burning piñon logs, turquoise mines, petroglyphs, the exciting people who came to visit, doing wonderful Native American arts and crafts, learning about all the plants and animals in the area, the summer camps, and most of all, Granddaddy's stories.

Then I thought about my family in California. I really missed my sister and my brother. I realized I only saw children in New Mexico during the summer. I did not go to school. Aunt Julie was a very good teacher, and she taught me at home. Although she and Granddaddy would have done anything for me, they lived in an adult world—and I was still a little girl. I yearned for friends and wanted to play with my siblings.

I decided to return home to California.

Seton and Aunt Julie

Taken by Willard Hoel of Lordsburg N.M. Jan 6, '34

CHAPTER 26

Leaving Santa Fe

Portion of Two-Bright-Eyes from *The Book of Woodcraft* by Ernest Thompson Seton

Although Granddaddy and Aunt Julie seemed very sad when I told them I had decided to go home to California with my parents, they accepted my decision and did not make any attempt to get me to change my mind. When it was time for me to leave, Granddaddy sat down on the steps and pulled me down next to him. "Time for one last brief story, Chipmunk. This one," he said, "is about a little Indian girl named Two-Bright-Eyes."

She was the only child of her parents. She wandered away one evening seeking the whippoorwill and got lost—you see, even Indians get lost sometimes. She never returned. The mourning parents never learned what became of her, but they thought they saw a new pair of twin stars rising through the trees not long after, and when their grief was so softened by time that they could sing about it, this is the song they made about their loss.

THE TWIN STARS

Two-Bright-Eyes went wandering out
To chase the whippoorwill.
Two-Bright-Eyes got lost, and left
Our teepee, oh, so still!

Two-Bright-Eyes was lifted up
To sparkle in the skies,
And look like stars, but we know well
That that's our lost Bright-Eyes,

She is looking for the camp,
She would come back if she could;
She is peeping thro' the trees to find
The teepee in the wood.

At the end of the story, Granddaddy gave me a huge bear hug and said, "Good-bye, darling Leila. You are my Two-Bright-Eyes." He then turned and walked into the house. I think this was his way of telling me how much he would miss me and that he understood my decision to return home.

I kissed Aunt Julie and clung to her, sobbing, until my mother came over, took my hand, and led me to the car. We drove away. I waved long after Aunt Julie appeared to be nothing more than a dot on the horizon. I went back to school, made new friends, resumed life with my brother and sister, and became a "city" girl. I wrote to Aunt Julie and Granddaddy often, but I was in San Francisco, where my family had moved during my absence, and over time, Santa Fe became a world away.

Memories dim, but in the many times I have thought back on those years, I have never underestimated the love I felt for Granddaddy and Aunt Julie or the love they had for me. I believe I always held a special place in their hearts, just as they have always held a special place in mine. My life with them helped shape my childhood and, in doing so, clearly influenced my adulthood. My memories of those years remain among those I most treasure.

My hope is that by writing this book, I have kindled an interest in Granddaddy's stories for my readers. If so, I will, in some small way, have repaid the debt I owe him and Aunt Julie for those unforgettable years.

To my chipmunk
from Grandaddy ~
which is Ernest *** Seton
óóó
29th nov 1934

To the
Chipmunk
with my heart's love ~

Aunt Julie ♀

AFTERWORD

SETON VILLAGE

HAS BEEN DESIGNATED A
REGISTERED NATIONAL
HISTORIC LANDMARK

UNDER THE PROVISIONS OF THE
HISTORIC SITES ACT OF AUGUST 21, 1935
THIS SITE POSSESSES EXCEPTIONAL VALUE
IN COMMEMORATING OR ILLUSTRATING
THE HISTORY OF THE UNITED STATES
U. S. DEPARTMENT OF THE INTERIOR
NATIONAL PARK SERVICE

1966

Granddady died in 1946 at the age of eighty-six. For two decades following his death, my aunt carried on the work they had for so many years done together, devoting time to writing and sustaining an active lecture schedule. Although much of the acreage of Seton Village was sold off, she continued to live in the Village and maintain the Castle and the area surrounding it until her death in 1975.

In December 1965, Seton Village was declared a Registered National Historic Landmark by the United States Department of the Interior. This was a true testament to the importance of all that Seton had accomplished in his lifetime.

In 1967, Aunt Julie, wishing to ensure that a substantial body of Seton's artwork and personal memorabilia would be maintained in perpetuity, gifted the contents of his personal library to the Boy Scouts of America. The donation included more than sixty thousand books, two of his most important oil paintings, hundreds of drawings, Seton's White Swan pictographs, and Lobo's pelt. This collection is housed at the Philmont Museum and Seton Memorial Library at the Philmont Scout Ranch in Cimarron, New Mexico. Portions of the collection are available for public viewing.

Dee Seton Barber (b. 1938), Granddaddy and Aunt Julie's adopted daughter, remained the foremost authority on Seton until her death in 2006. She resided at Seton Castle until relocating to

Tennessee in 2000. In 2003, she sold the Castle, part of the contents of the house, and the remaining eighty-six acres of land to the Academy for the Love of Learning. The Academy undertook the restoration of the Castle, but its work came to a halt after a construction-related fire destroyed a large part of the structure in 2005. In spite of the serious damage, the Academy persevered with its work and, through collaboration with architects and engineers, arrived at a plan to strengthen and restore the exterior of the building. Fortunately, drawings, books, and other archival materials had been removed from the house and placed in storage prior to the fire.

The Castle, with its newly constructed façade, has been open for public touring since 2011. A number of Seton's paintings and drawings are available for viewing in the Seton Gallery and Archives located adjacent to the Castle in the beautiful, environmentally-sensitive Academy for the Love of Learning building.

Seton Castle restoration

A SELECTION OF CHILDREN'S BOOKS BY ERNEST THOMPSON SETON

Animal Heroes, Scribners (1905)
  "The Slum Cat"
  "Arnaux: The Chronicles of a Homing Pigeon"
  "Badlands Billy: The Wolf that Won"
  "The Boy and the Lynx"
  "Little Warhorse: The History of a Jack-rabbit"
  "Snap: The Story of a Bull-terrier"
  "The Winnipeg Wolf"
  "The Legend of the White Reindeer"

Bannertail: The Story of a Gray Squirrel, Scribners (1922)

The Biography of a Grizzly, Century (1900)

The Book of Woodcraft and Indian Lore, Doubleday, Page & Co., 590 pp. More than 500 drawings by the author; 3rd edition of the 1912 issue, enlarged by the inclusion of "The Foresters Manual" (1922).

Lives of the Hunted, Scribners (1901)
  "Krag the Kootenay Ram"
  "A Street Troubadour: Being the Adventures of a Cock Sparrow"
  "Johnny Bear"
  "The Mother Teal and the Overland Route"
  "Chink: The Development of a Pup"
  "The Kangaroo Rat"
  "Tito: The Story of the Coyote that Learned How"
  "Why the Chickadee Goes Crazy Once a Year"

Lobo, Rag, and Vixen, Scribners (1899)

Monarch, The Big Bear of Tallac, Scribners (1904)

Rolf in the Woods, Doubleday (Dedicated to the Boy Scouts of America) (1911)

The Trail of the Sandhill Stag, Scribners (1899)

Two Little Savages, Doubleday (1903)

The Wild Animal Play for Children (Musical), Doubleday & Curtis (1900)

Wild Animals I Have Known, Scribners (1898)
    "Lobo, the King of Currumpaw"
    "Silverspot, the Story of a Crow"
    "Raggylug, the Story of a Cottontail Rabbit"
    "Bingo, the Story of My Dog"
    "The Springfield Fox"
    "The Prancing Mustang"
    "Wully, the Story of a Yaller Dog"
    "Redruff the Story of the Don Valley Partridge"

ACKNOWLEDGEMENTS AND NOTES

Cover art – Michael Harrison Tyrrell. *The Storyteller*. 2012. Pen, ink and tempera paint. Private collection of Leila Moss Knox.

Front Material

Page ii, photograph – Kellogg, Harold Evans. *Ernest Thompson Seton*. Santa Fe, NM. c.1940. Blue Sky: The Ernest Thompson Seton Pages. Web. 12 April 2012. Courtesy of Blue Sky: The Ernest Thompson Seton Pages. <etsetoninstitute.org>.

Page v, photograph – Peacock Tile on the Wall of Seton Castle, Santa Fe, NM. 2010. From the private collection of Linda L. Knox.

Page vii, drawing – Seton, Ernest Thompson. "Johnny Bear." *Lives of the Hunted: Containing a True Account of the Doings of Five Quadrupeds & Three Birds, and in Elucidation of the Same, over 200 Drawings*. New York: Charles Scribner's Sons, 1901. 173. Print.

Page ix, drawing – Seton, Ernest Thompson. *Drums and Shields*. c. 1920s. Pen and ink. Image 546. Academy for the Love of Learning, Santa Fe, NM. Courtesy Academy for the Love of Learning.

Page xiii, portrait – Rhead, Louis. *To Ernest Thompson Seton with thanks & admiration of his works*. N.d. Image 502. Academy for the Love of Learning, Santa Fe, NM. Courtesy Academy for the Love of Learning.

Prologue

Page 1, drawing – Seton, Ernest Thompson. *Drawing of Seton Castle, 1935*. Reproduced from Seton, Julia M. Buttree. *By a Thousand Fires: Nature Notes and Extracts from the Life and Unpublished Journals of Ernest Thompson Seton*. Garden City, NY: Doubleday & Company, 1967. Print. Courtesy the Seton Family Trust.

Chapter 1 — From Los Angeles to Santa Fe

Page 2, drawing – Seton, Ernest Thompson. *Drawing of Seton Castle, 1935*. Reproduced from Seton, Julia M. Buttree. *By a Thousand Fires: Nature Notes and Extracts from the Life and Unpublished Journals of Ernest Thompson Seton*. Garden City, NY: Doubleday & Company, 1967. Print. Courtesy the Seton Family Trust.

Page 4, map – Tyrrell, Michael Harrison. *Leila's trip from Los Angeles, Caliornia to Santa Fe, New Mexico*. 2013. Pen, ink and tempera paint. Private collection of Leila Moss Knox

Page 7, photograph – *Ernest Thompson Seton & Leila Moss (Knox)*. c. 1932. Santa Fe, NM. From the private collection of Leila Moss Knox.

Chapter 2 — Lots of "Oldest" in Santa Fe

Page 8, photograph (top) – *La Fonda on the Plaza*. c. 1930s. La Fonda, Santa Fe, NM. La Fonda on the Plaza. Web. 12 April 2012. Photo provided, with permission, by La Fonda on the Plaza, Santa Fe, NM.
<www.lafondasantafe.com>.

Page 8, photograph (bottom) – Prezelpaws. *Santa Fe San Miguel Chapel* 2002. *Wikimedia Commons*. Web. 8 April 2014. Used courtesy of the photographer under the terms of the GNU Free Documentation License, Version 1.2 or later.
<commons.wikimedia.org/wiki/File:Santa_Fe_San_miguel_chapel.jpg>.

Page 9, map – Holdred, Doug. *Santa Fe Trail*. N.d. *Santa Fe Trail Association*. Web. 24 April 2012. Image by Doug Holdred. Courtesy of the Santa Fe Trail Association.
<www.santafetrail.org/mapping-marking/trail-maps/>.

Page 10, top photograph – Parkhurst, T. Harmon. *Pueblo Indians selling pottery and jewelry on portal, Palace of the Governors, Santa Fe, NM*. c. 1925–1945. "Photo Archives – T. Harmon Parkhurst Photo Collection". *Palace of the Governors*. Palace of the Governors/New Mexico History Museum, Santa Fe, NM. Web. 4.12.12. <econtent.unm.edu/cdm/ref/collection/parkhurst/id/3586>. T. Harmon Parkhurst, Courtesy Palace of the Governors Photo Archives (NMHM/DCA), negative number 069973.

Page 10, bottom photo – Curtis, Edward S. *The Blanket Weaver–Navajo*. c. 1905. Web. 14 November 2013. Public domain photo. Library of Congress. Prints & Photographs Division, Edward S. Curtis Collection, reproduction number LOT 12311, LC-USZ62-116675 (b&w film copy negative). <http://www.loc.gov/pictures/item/96514456/>.

Page 11, photograph – Kvaran, Einar Einarsson. *New Mexico Palace Santa Fe* (Palace of the Governors). 2004. *Wikimedia Commons*. Web. 8 April 2014. Used courtesy of the photographer under the terms of the GNU Free Documentation License, Version 1.2 or later.
<commons.wikimedia.org/wiki/File:NewMexicoPalaceSantaFe.jpg>.

Chapter 3 — How I Came to Be Called "Chipmunk"

Page 13, drawing – Seton, Ernest Thompson. *Chipmunks for Life, 1892* (detail). 1892. Pen and Ink. Philmont Museum-Seton Memorial Library, Cimarron, NM. Image courtesy of Philmont Museum-Seton Memorial Library, Cimarron, NM. A gift of Mrs. Julia M. Seton and the Seton family.

Chapter 4 — Granddaddy's Stories

Page 14, photograph (left) – *Publicity Shot of Ernest Thompson Seton*. New York. 1906. Philmont Museum-Seton Memorial Library, Cimarron, NM. Image courtesy of Philmont Museum-Seton Memorial Library, Cimarron, NM. A gift of Mrs. Julia M. Seton and the Seton family.

Page 14, photograph (center) – Edmonds, Ron. *Ernest Thompson Seton signature plate. Blue Sky: The Ernest Thompson Seton Pages*. N.p., n.d. Web. 22 April 2012. Courtesy of Ron Edmonds, Blue Sky: The Ernest Thompson Seton Pages,

Page 14, cover image (right) – Seton, Ernest Thompson. *Wild Animals I Have Known*. New York: Charles Scribner's Sons, 1912. Print.

Chapter 5 — "Raggylug, The Story of a Cottontail Rabbit"

Pages 15–17, story excerpt - Seton, Ernest Thompson. "Raggylug, The Story of a Cottontail Rabbit." *Wild Animals I Have Known and 200 Drawings*. New York: Grosset & Dunlap by arrangement with Charles Scribner's Son, 1898. 93–100. Print.

Page 16, drawing – *Wild Animals I Have Known*, 97.

Page 17, drawing –*Wild Animals I Have Known*, 105.

Chapter 6 — Evening Drives

Page 18, photograph (top) – Witt, David L. *Sangre de Cristo Mountains*. 2010. New Mexico. Used courtesy of the photographer.

Page 18, photograph (bottom) – Witt, David L. *Piñon Tree, Seton Village*. 2012. New Mexico. Used courtesy of the photographer.

Page 19, photograph – Dncsn, J. *Dried Flowers – Decoration 3*. 2009. *Wikimedia Commons*. Web. 8 April 2014. Used under the terms of the GNU Free Documentation License, Version 1.2 or later. <commons.wikimedia.org/wiki/File%3ADried_flowers_-_decoration_3.jpg>.

Page 20, photograph (top left) – Witt, David L. *Santa Fe Phlox*. c. 2000s. New Mexico. Used courtesy of the photographer.

Page 20, photograph (top center) – Witt, David L. *Dakota Vervain*. c. 2000s. New Mexico. Used courtesy of the photographer.

Page 20, photograph (top right) – Witt, David L. *Hairy Golden Aster*. New Mexico. c. 2000s. Used courtesy of the photographer.

Page 20, photograph (bottom left) – Witt, David L. *Buffalo Gourd*. New Mexico. c. 2000s. Used courtesy of the photographer.

Page 20, photograph (bottom center) – Witt, David L. *Banana Yucca*. New Mexico. c. 2000s. Used courtesy of the photographer.

Page 20, photograph (bottom right) – Witt, David L. *Claret Cup Cactus*. New Mexico. c. 2000s. Used courtesy of the photographer.

Chapter 7 — Trailing

Page 21–23, excerpts – Seton, Ernest Thompson. *The Book of Woodcraft and Indian Lore with Over 500 Drawings by the Author*. Garden City, NY: Doubleday, Page & Company, 1912. 370–375. Print.

Page 22, drawing – Seton, Ernest Thompson. *The Book of Woodcraft*, 374.

Page 23, drawing – Seton, Ernest Thompson. "Badlands Billy." *Animal Heroes: Being the Histories of a Cat, a Dog, a Pigeon, a Lynx, Two Wolves & a Reindeer and in Eulucidation of the Same over 200 Drawings.* Every Boy's Library – Boy Scout Edition. New York: Grosset & Dunlap by arrangement with Charles Scribner's Sons, 1905. 151. Print.

Chapter 8 — "The Cat and the Skunk"

Pages 24–27, story excerpts – Seton, Ernest Thompson. "The Cat and the Skunk." *Two Little Savages: Being the Adventures of Two Boys Who Lived as Indians and What They Learned.* Garden City, NY: Doubleday, Page & Company, 1903. 327–336. Print.

Page 24, drawing – *Two Little Savages,* 327.

Page 26, drawing – Seton, Ernest Thompson. "Badlands Billy." *Animal Heroes: Being the Histories of a Cat, a Dog, a Pigeon, a Lynx, Two Wolves & a Reindeer and in Eulucidation of the Same over 200 Drawings.* Every Boy's Library – Boy Scout Edition. New York: Grosset & Dunlap by arrangement with Charles Scribner's Sons, 1905. 125. Print.

Page 27, drawing – *Two Little Savages,* 333.

Chapter 9 — A Porcupine Hunt

Page 28, drawing – "Porcupine." *Wikimedia Commons.* 2007. Web. 8 April 2014. Released into public domain by Pearson Scott Foresman, publisher. <commons.wikimedia.org/wiki/File:Porcupine_(PSF).png>.

Page 29, drawing – Jomegat. Tracks left by *Erethizon dorsatum* (porcupine). 2008. Web. 8 April 2014. Permission is granted to copy, distribute, and/or modify under the terms of the GNU Free Documentation License, Version 1.2 or any later version. <commons.wikimedia.org/wiki/File:Porcupine_tracks.png>.

Page 30, number of quills on a porcupine – Seton, Julia M. *By a Thousand Fires: Nature Notes and Extracts from the Life and Unpublished Journals of Ernest Thompson Seton.* Garden City, NY: Doubleday, 1967. 81. Print.

Page 30, drawing (top) – Seton, Ernest Thompson. *Moccasins (of Gym-Shoes).* N.d. Watercolor and pen & ink. Image 553. Academy for the Love of Learning, Santa Fe, NM. Courtesy Academy for the Love of Learning.

Page 30, drawing (bottom) – Seton, Ernest Thompson. *Moccasins Made of Sneaks.* N.d. Watercolor and pen & ink. Image 550. Academy for the Love of Learning, Santa Fe, NM. Courtesy Academy for the Love of Learning.

Page 31, painting – Seton, Ernest Thompson. *Untitled warbonnet.* N.d. Image 548. Academy for the Love of Learning, Santa Fe, NM. Courtesy Academy for the Love of Learning.

Chapter 10 — "The Foundling"

Pages 32–33, story excerpt – Seton, Ernest Thompson. *Bannertail: The Story of a Graysquirrel.* New York: Charles Scribner's Sons, 1922. 3–7. Print.

Page 32, drawing – *Bannertail,* 28.

Page 33, drawing – *Bannertail,* following 12.

Chapter 11 — A Valuable Lesson

Page 35, drawing – Seton, Ernest Thompson. Untitled Row of Animals. N.d. Pen and ink. Image 976. Academy for the Love of Learning, Santa Fe, NM. Courtesy Academy for the Love of Learning.

Chapter 12 — "Why the Chickadee Goes Crazy Once a Year"

Pages 36–38, story – Seton, Ernest Thompson. "Why the Chickadee Goes Crazy Once a Year." *Lives of the Hunted: Containing a True Account of the Doings of Five Quadrupeds & Three Birds, and in Elucidation of the Same, over 200 Drawings.* New York: Charles Scribner's Sons, 1901. 355–360. Print.

Page 36, drawing – Seton, Ernest Thompson. *The Book of Woodcraft and Indian Lore with Over 500 Drawings by the Author.* Garden City, NY: Doubleday, Page & Company, 1912. 250. Print.

Page 37, drawing – *Lives of the Hunted,* 355.

Chapter 13 — The College of Indian Wisdom

Pages 40–43, information on pictographs and handsigns – Seton, Ernest Thompson. *The Book of Woodcraft and Indian Lore with Over 500 Drawings by the Author.* Garden City, NY: Doubleday, Page & Company, 1912. 228–244. Print.

Page 39 – Seton, Ernest Thompson. *Seton Institute Map* (close up). N.d. Ink, watercolor & colored pencil. Image 1001. Academy for the Love of Learning, Santa Fe, NM. Courtesy Academy for the Love of Learning.

Page 40, photograph (top) – *Leila Moss (Knox), Santa Fe, NM.* c. 1930s. From the private collection of Leila Moss Knox.

Page 40, photograph (bottom) – *Mrs. Ernest Thompson Seton in lecture costume.* c. 1935. *Palace of the Governors.* Web. 12 April 2012. <econtent.unm.edu/cdm/singleitem/collection/acpa/id/3910>. Photographer unknown. Courtesy Palace of the Governors Photo Archives, (NMHM/DCA); negative number 050468.

Page 41, information on handsigns – *The Book of Woodcraft,* 229–231.

Page 42, drawing – *The Book of Woodcraft,* 244.

Page 43, drawing – *The Book of Woodcraft,* 242–243.

Chapter 14 — "Lobo, the King of the Currumpaw"

Pages 44–49, story excerpt – Seton, Ernest Thompson. "Lobo, The King of Currumpaw." *Wild Animals I Have Known and 200 Drawings.* New York: Grosset & Dunlap, published by arrangement with Charles Scribner's Sons, 1898. 17–54. Print.

Page 44, drawing – Seton, Ernest Thompson. *Untitled Wolf Head.* N.d. Pen and ink. Image 538. Academy for the Love of Learning, Santa Fe, NM. Courtesy Academy for the Love of Learning.

Page 46, drawing – *Wild Animals I Have Known,* 45.

Page 49, drawing of Lobo and Blanca – *Wild Animals I Have Known,* 42.

Chapter 15 — Personal Best

Page 50, drawing – Seton, Ernest Thompson. "Tito." *Lives of the Hunted: Containing a True Account of the Doings of Five Quadrupeds & Three Birds, and in Elucidation of the Same, over 200 Drawings.* New York: Charles Scribner's Sons, 1901. 311. Print.

Page 52, photograph – *Seton and Julie in New Mexico.* 1927. Academy for the Love of Learning, Santa Fe, NM. Courtesy Academy for the Love of Learning.

Chapter 16 — Plays at Childervil

Pages 53–54, script excerpt – Seton, Ernest Thompson. *The Wild Animal Play for Children with Alternate Reading for Very Young Children.* New York: Doubleday, Page & Company, 1900. 52–55. Print.

Page 53, drawing – *The Wild Animal Play for Children,* 57.

Page 54, drawing – *The Wild Animal Play for Children,* 56.

Chapter 17 — Memory Hill

Pages 55–57, information on Native American dances, fire lighting and personalities – Seton, Ernest Thompson. *The Book of Woodcraft and Indian Lore with Over 500 Drawings by the Author.* Garden City, NY: Doubleday, Page & Company, 1912. 158 (Ojibwa Snake Dance), 192–194 (fire lighting), 485 (Winnemucca). Print.

Page 55, cover image – Seton, Ernest Thompson. *The Birch-bark Roll of the Woodcraft Indians Containing Their Constitution, Laws, Games and Deeds.* Garden City, NY: Doubleday, Page & Company, 1906. Cover. Print.

Page 56, drawing – *The Book of Woodcraft,* 194.

Page 57, drawing – Seton, Ernest Thompson. *Dancing Frieze.* 1939. Pen and ink. Image 104. Academy for the Love of Learning, Santa Fe, NM. Courtesy Academy for the Love of Learning.

Page 58, drawing – Seton, Ernest Thompson. *Untitled Pipes.* c. 1920s. Ink and pencil/paper. Image 554. Academy for the Love of Learning, Santa Fe, NM. Courtesy Academy for the Love of Learning.

Chapter 18 — The Wonders of New Mexico

Pages 61–64, story excerpt – Seton, Ernest Thompson. "Atalapha." *Wild Animal Ways*. Garden City, NY: Doubleday, Page, & Company 1917. 150–153. Print.

Page 60, drawing – Seton, Ernest Thompson. *V(espertilo). Subulatus (bat)*. 1882. Pen and ink on paper board. Image 518. Academy for the Love of Learning, Santa Fe, NM. Courtesy Academy for the Love of Learning.

Page 62, drawing – *Wild Animal Ways*, 160.

Page 64, photographs – Acoma Pueblo, NM. 2010. From the private collection of Linda L. Knox.

Pages 65–66, myth excerpt – Stirling, Matthew Williams. *Origin Myth of Acoma and Other Records*. Washington: U.S. G.P.O., 1942. Print. Smithsonian Institution, Bureau of American Ethnology Bulletin 135. 1–123. Courtesy the Smithsonian Institution.

Page 67, photographs – Tyrrell, Michael Harrison. *Petroglyphs, Petrotoglyph National Monument, NM*. 2010. Courtesy of the photographer.

Page 68, photographs – Baxter, W. Cerrillos Hills State Park, New Mexico. Web. 1 May 2012. Courtesy of the photographer. <www.emnrd.state.nm.us/SPD/cerrilloshillsstatepark.html>.

Chapter 19 — Quicksight and the Moccasin Game

Page 69, drawing – Seton, Ernest Thompson. *The Book of Woodcraft and Indian Lore with Over 500 Drawings by the Author*. Garden City, NY: Doubleday, Page & Company. 1912. 291. Print.

Pages 70–71, Poem – Brown, Howard Clark (a.k.a. Tokinaya). "The Moccasin Game." *Child Life in Seton Village*. La Grange, IL: Ever-Redi Printing Service, 1949. Print.

Pages 70–71, drawings – Seton, Ernest Thompson. *Teepees* (detail). N.d. Academy for the Love of Learning, Santa Fe, NM. Courtesy Academy for the Love of Learning.

Chapter 20 — On the Road: Beyond New Mexico

Page 72, drawing – Seton, Ernest Thompson. *Untitled Row of Teepees*. N.d. Image 942. The Academy for the Love of Learning, Santa Fe, NM. Courtesy Academy for the Love of Learning.

Chapter 21 — "The Slum Cat"

Pages 74–76, story excerpt – Seton, Ernest Thompson. "The Slum Cat." *Animal Heroes: Being the Histories of a Cat, a Dog, a Pigeon, a Lynx, Two Wolves & a Reindeer and in Elucidation of the Same over 200 Drawings*. Every Boy's Library – Boy Scout Edition. New York: Grosset & Dunlap by arrangement with Charles Scribner's Sons, 1905. 25–31. Print.

Page 74, drawing – *Animal Heroes*, 16.

Page 75, drawing – *Animal Heroes*, 20.

Page 76, drawing (large) – *Animal Heroes*, 27.

Page 76, drawing (small) – *Animal Heroes*, 47.

Chapter 22 — Hogan and Kiva

Page 77, drawing (top) – Seton, Ernest Thompson. *Painted Paddles by Woodcrafters*. N.d. Watercolor and pen & ink. Image 551. Academy for the Love of Learning, Santa Fe, NM. Courtesy Academy for the Love of Learning.

Page 77, drawing (bottom) – Seton, Ernest Thompson. *Woodcraft Designs for Canoes*. c. 1920s. Watercolor and pen & ink. Image 549. Academy for the Love of Learning, Santa Fe, NM. Courtesy Academy for the Love of Learning.

Page 78, photograph (top) – PRA, photographer. *Hogan Navajo*. N.p. 2007. Web. 5 March 2012. Used courtesy of the photographer under the terms of the GNU Free Documentation License, Version 1.2 or later. <en.wikipedia.or/wiki/File:Hogan_Navajo.jpg>.

Page 78, photograph (bottom) – Kiva at Acoma Pueblo, NM. 2010. From the private collection of Linda L. Knox.

Page 79, journal page – Seton, Ernest Thompson. *Unpublished Journal*. New Mexico. 1933. Rare Book Collection at the American Museum of Natural History, New York. Print. Photographic image courtesy of the American Museum of Natural History.

Page 80, photograph (top) – Smith, Bettylu Knox. *Seton Village Hogan*, Santa Fe, NM. 2010. Courtesy of the photographer.

Page 80, photograph (bottom) – Tyrrell, Michael Harrison. *Seton Village Kiva*, Sante Fe, NM. 2010. Courtesy of the photographer.

Chapter 23 — "Johnny Bear"

Pages 81–85, story excerpt – Seton, Ernest Thompson. "Johnny Bear." *Lives of the Hunted: Containing a True Account of the Doings of Five Quadrupeds & Three Birds, and in Elucidation of the Same, over 200 Drawings*. New York: Charles Scribner's Sons, 1901, 141–176. Print.

Page 82, drawing – *Lives of the Hunted*, 159.

Page 83, drawing – *Lives of the Hunted*, 176.

Page 84, drawing – *Lives of the Hunted*, 142.

Page 85, drawing – *Lives of the Hunted*, 164.

Chapter 24 — Visitors to the Castle

Page 86, photograph (top left) – Davis, Wyatt. *Maria Martinez applying a fine slip surface to a pot, San Ildefonso Pueblo, New Mexico*. 1938. *Palace of the Governors*. Photo Archives Collection (NMHM/DCA), negative 050086. Santa Fe, NM: Palace of the Governors/The New Mexico History Museum, 2011. Web. 4 May 2012. <econtent.unm.edu/cdm/singleitem/collection/acpa/id/8882/rec/73>. Wyatt Davis, Courtesy Palace of Governors Photo Archives (NMHM/DCA), negative 050086.

Page 86, Photograph (center right) – Lummis, Charles Fletcher. *Mary Hunter Austin ca. 1900.* *Wikimedia Commons.* Web. 8 April 2014. Image is in public domain because its copyright has expired. <commons.wikimedia.org/wiki/File:Mary_Austin_c.1900.jpg>.

Page 86, photograph (bottom left) – *Kiowa Indian Jack Hokeah - American Indian Exposition - Anadarko Oklahoma.* 1944. *Oklahoma Historical Society Research Division.* Pierre Tartoue Collection: Photographs, Box 1, 19261.6.A. Oklahoma Historical Society. Web. 10 April 2012. <www.okhistory.org/research/photos?full>. Courtesy Research Division of the Oklahoma Historical Society.

Page 87, photograph (top right) – *Te Ata.* N.d. Photograph. Chickasaw Nation Museum and Libraries: Division of History and Culture. Photo courtesy of the Chickasaw Nation Archives.

Page 87, photograph (center left) – *Gerald Cassidy with his painting "Navajo Romance" which was purchased by the French Government for the Luxembourg Galleries in Paris.* N.d. *Palace of the Governors:* Photo Archives Collection (NMHM/DCA), negative 007121. Santa Fe, NM: Palace of the Governors/The New Mexico History Museum, 2006. Web. 16 April 2012. <econtent.unm.edu/cdm/singleitem/collection/acpa/id/27/rec/11>. Photographer unknown. Courtesy Palace of Governors Photo Archives (NMHM/DCA), negative 007121.

Page 87, photograph of Clement Hull (bottom right) – *Van Briggle Artist.* 1948. *Wikipedia.* Web. 8 April 2014. Photo has been released into Pubic Domain. <en.wikipedia.org/wiki/File:Van-Briggle-Artist.jpg>.

Chapter 25 — To Stay or Not to Stay

Page 88, photograph – Holt, Willard. *Ernest Thompson Seton and Julia Seton, Jan 10, '34.* Located in Seton, Ernest Thompson. *Unpublished Journal.* New Mexico. 1934. Print. Journal is in the Rare Book Collection at the American Museum of Natural History, New York. Photographic image courtesy of the American Museum of Natural History.

Chapter 26 — Leaving Santa Fe

Page 89, story and poem excerpt – Related in Seton, Ernest Thompson. "Two-Bright Eyes." *The Book of Woodcraft and Indian Lore With Over 500 Drawings by the Author.* Garden City, NY: Doubleday, Page & Company, 1912. 211. Print.

Page 91, autograph – Granddaddy's signature in Leila's autograph book. 1934. From the private collection of Leila Moss Knox.

Page 91, autograph – Aunt Julie's signature in Leila's autograph book. 1934. From the private collection of Leila Moss Knox.

Afterword

Page 92, photograph – Tyrrell, Michael Harrison. *Historical Landmark Plaque at Seton Village, NM.* 2010. Used courtesy of the photographer.

Page 93, photograph – Tyrrell, Michael Harrison. *Seton Castle after Restoration, NM.* 2012. Used courtesy of the photographer.

A Selection of Children's Books by Ernest Thompson Seton

Page 94, cover image – Seton, Ernest Thompson Seton. *Wild Animals at Home.* Garden City, NY: Doubleday, Page & Co., 1913.

Page 94, cover image – Seton, Ernest Thompson. *Two Little Savages.* New York: Grosset & Dunlap, 1911.

Page 94, cover image – Seton, Ernest Thompson. *Biography of a Silver Fox.* New York: The Century Company, New York, 1908.

Page 94, cover image – Seton, Ernest Thompson. *Wild Animals at Home.* New York: Grosset & Dunlap, 1913.

Page 94, cover image – Seton, Ernest Thompson. *The Woodcraft Manual for Girls.* Garden City, NY: Doubleday, Page & Co, 1916.

Page 94, cover image – Seton, Ernest Thompson. *Lives of the Hunted.* New York: Charles Scribner's Sons, 1901.

Page 95, cover image – Seton, Ernest Thompson. *Wild Animals I Have Known.* New York: Charles Scribner's Sons, 1901.

Page 95, cover image – Seton, Ernest Thompson. *The Biography of a Grizzly.* New York: The Century Company, 1900.

Page 95, cover image – Seton, Ernest Thompson. *Bannertail, The Story of a Graysquirrel.* New York: Charles Scribner's Sons, 1922.

Page 95, cover image – Seton, Ernest Thompson. *Lobo, Rag & Vixen.* New York: Charles Scribner's Sons, 1899.

Page 95, cover image – Seton, Ernest Thompson. *Monarch, the Big Bear [of Tallac].* New York: Charles Scribner's Sons, 1904.

Page 95, cover image – Seton, Ernest Thompson. *The Arctic Prairies: A Canoe-Journey of 2,000 Miles in Search of the Caribou.* New York: Charles Scribner's Sons, 1920.

Acknowledgements

Page 105, title page – Seton, Ernest Thompson. *The Biography of a Grizzly.* New York: The Century Company, 1900.

Page 105, title page – Seton, Ernest Thompson. *Two Little Savages.* Garden City, NY: Doubleday, Page & Company, 1903.

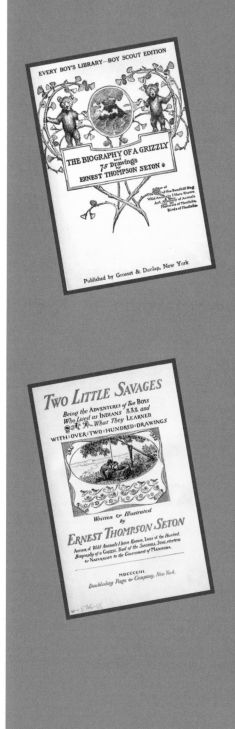

BIBLIOGRAPHY

"About La Fonda on the Plaza." *La Fonda on The Plaza.* Santa Fe, NM, n.d. Web. 08 Apr. 2014.
     <www.lafondasantafe.com/about-la-fonda/>.

"Acoma Pueblo." *Sky City Cultural Center & Haak'u Museum.* Acoma Pueblo, NM, n.d. Web. 8 Apr. 2014.
     <www.acomaskycity.org/home.html>.

Austin, Mary. *Literary America, 1903-1934: The Mary Austin Letters.* Ed. T. M. Pearce. Westport, CT:
     Greenwood, 1979. Print.

Brown, Howard Clark (a.k.a. Tokinaya). *Child Life in Seton Village.* La Grange, IL: Ever-Redi Printing
     Service, 1949. Print.

Buttree, Julia M (a.k.a. Julia Seton). *The Rhythm of the Redman.* New York: A.S. Barnes and Company
     Incorporated, 1930. Print.

"Clement Marot Hull: Master Potter: Biography." *Clement Marot Hull: A Van Briggle Original.* N.p., n.d.
     Web. 08 Apr. 2014. <www.clemhull.com/>.

Edmonds, Ron. *Blue Sky: The Ernest Thompson Seton Pages.* N.p., n.d. Web. 8 April 2014.
     .

Green, Richard. *Te Ata: Chickasaw Storyteller, American Treasure.* Norman: University of Oklahoma,
     2002. Print.

Marriott, Alice. *Maria: The Potter of San Ildefonso.* Norman: University of Oklahoma Press, 1948. Print.
     The Civilization of the American Indian, Vol. 27.

Milford, Homer. "Turquoise Mining History." *Amigos de Cerrillos Hills State Park.* Cerrillos, NM, Amigos
     de Cerrillos Hills State Park, 2014. Web. 8 April 2014.
     <www.cerrilloshills.org/history/turquoise-mining-history>.

Myers, Harry C. "A History of the Santa Fe Trail." *Official Santa Fe Trail Association.* Santa Fe Trail
     Association, Larned, KS, 2010. Web. 8 Apr. 2014.
     <www.santafetrail.org/the-trail/history/history-of-the-sft/>.

O'Hern, John. "The Inn at the End of the Trail." *Western Art Collector.* Dec. 2011: 50-55. Print.

Seton, Ernest Thompson. *Animal Heroes: Being the Histories of a Cat, a Dog, a Pigeon, a Lynx, Two Wolves
     & a Reindeer and in Eulucidation of the Same over 200 Drawings.* Every Boy's Library – Boy Scout
     Edition. New York: Grosset & Dunlap by arrangement with Charles Scribner's Sons, 1905. Print.

---. *Bannertail: The Story of a Grayquirrel.* New York: Charles Scribner's Sons, 1922. Print.

---. *The Book of Woodcraft and Indian Lore with Over 500 Drawings by the Author.* Garden City, NY:
     Doubleday, Page & Company, 1912. Print.

---. *Lives of the Hunted: Containing a True Account of the Doings of Five Quadrupeds & Three Birds, and in
     Elucidation of the Same, over 200 Drawings.* New York: Charles Scribner's Sons, 1901. Print.

---. *Two Little Savages: Being the Adventures of Two Boys Who Lived as Indians and What They Learned.* New York: Doubleday, Page & Company, 1903. Print.

---. *Unpublished Journals, 1930-1936.* N.p, Print. Journals are unpublished volumes; those from 1930 to 1936 were largely written in Seton Village, NM. Journals are in the Rare Book Collection at the American Museum of Natural History, New York.

---. *The Wild Animal Play for Children, with Alternate Reading for Very Young Children.* Garden City, NY: Doubleday, Page & Company, 1900. Print.

---. *Wild Animal Ways.* Garden City, NY: Doubleday, Page & Company, 1916. Print.

---. *Wild Animals I Have Known: And 200 Drawings.* New York: Grosset & Dunlap by arrangement with Charles Scribner's Sons, 1898. Print.

Seton, Julia M. Buttree. *By a Thousand Fires; Nature Notes and Extracts from the Life and Unpublished Journals of Ernest Thompson Seton.* Garden City, NY: Doubleday & Company, 1967. Print.

Stirling, Matthew Williams. *Origin Myth of Acoma, and Other Records.* Washington: U.S. G.P.O., 1942. Print. Smithsonian Institution Bureau of American Ethnology Bulletin 135: 1-123.

United States National Park Service. A*bout Bats, Caves, & Deserts: A Curriculum and Activity Guide for Carlsbad Caverns National Park.* U.S. Department of the Interior, 03 Apr. 2014. Web. 08 Apr. 2014. <www.nps.gov/cave/forteachers/abcd_curriculum.htm>.

United States National Park Service. "Petroglyph National Monument, New Mexico." U.S. Department of the Interior, 02 Apr. 2014. Web. 8 Apr. 2014. <www.nps.gov/petr/planyourvisit/def.htm>.

Watson, Mary Jo. "Jack Hokeah (ca. 1902-1969)." *Encyclopedia of Oklahoma History and Culture.* Oklahoma Historical Society, n.d. Web. 8 Apr. 2014. <digital.library.okstate.edu/encyclopedia/entries/H/HO009.html>.

Witt, David L. *Ernest Thompson Seton: The Life and Legacy of an Artist and Conservationist.* Layton, UT: Gibbs Smith, 2010. Print.

Witt, David L. and others. *Seton Legacy.* Academy for the Love of Learning, Santa Fe, NM. n.d. Web. 8 April 2014. <etsetoninstitute.org/>.